DAVID SCARPETA

HIDDEN BATTLES

The struggles you carry inside that no one knows

The mission of Editorial Vida is to be the leading company in meeting people's needs with resources whose content glorifies the Lord Jesus Christ and promotes biblical principles.

HIDDEN BATTLES
Published by Editorial Vida – 2026
Nashville, Tennessee

This title is also available in electronic and audio formats.

Interior design: Juan Shimabukuro
Illustrations: Juan Shimabukuro, Jackson Santamaria, and freepik.com

HarperCollins Publishers, Macken House, 39/40 Mayor Street Upper, Dublin 1, D01 C9W8, Ireland (https://www.harpercollins.com).

ISBN: 978-0-82977-5-006
eBook: 978-0-82977-5-013
Audio: 978-0-82977-5-020

Information regarding classification in the Library of Congress is available upon request.

CATEGORY: Religion / Christian Life / Spiritual Growth

PRINTED IN THE UNITED STATES OF AMERICA

26 27 28 29 30 LBC 5 4 3 2 1

You need this book — the great news is that you can win the Hidden Battles in your life! Pastor David Scarpeta will help you find the victory, so that you can be all that God has created you to be. This book is full of biblical, battle-tested strategies you can use today to win every day. David's encouraging voice will keep you going in the fight and cheer you on at the finish line. I've had the great blessing of seeing David live out the message he shares here in his own life, and I know this book can help you. Get it, read it, live it and share it — and discover God's incredible destiny for you.

Dr. Garrett Booth, Senior Pastor, Grace Church Houston

There is a battle between your mind and the face you show the world, between your struggles and what you let others see, between your lived story and your destiny. Pastor David Scarpeta, my beloved brother and friend, gives us a biblical path for emerging victorious from each of our own hidden battles. "This book isn't just meant to be read—it's meant to be lived."

Samuel Rodriguez, lead pastor of New Season, president of NHCLC, author of *Your Mess, God's Miracle!*, **executive producer of the films** *Breakthrough* **and** *Flamin, Hot*

I have a recommendation for you: the new book by my good friend Pastor David Scarpeta. I know the author well—along with his beautiful family and his growing church—and I am confident that David not only preaches the biblical truths masterfully embodied in this work, but, more importantly, applies them to his own life. For this reason, it has not been a surprise to me that he has been able to inspire and aid so many people around the world to conquer their Hidden Battles.

Sergio Hornung, Lead pastor of the Agua Viva church

ACKNOWLEDGMENTS

First, to my Heavenly Father, my Lord and Savior Jesus Christ and to the sweet Holy Spirit, how beautiful is life with You, my God.

You have walked by my side in all these battles and have given me victory in every one.

To my wife Diana, companion in battles, Love, thank you for walking by my side. You are a creative, resilient, patient woman. It is a blessing to live life with you.

To my four children: Daniela, my hero; Natanael, an incredible and visionary man; Jonathan, a boy full of life; and Elijah, a tender and loving child. How beautiful it is to be your papa!

To the church I serve as pastor, Grace Español Houston, for your patience and love for me and my family. Thank you for being a church after the heart of God. It is an honor to be your pastor.

To everyone who has been a part of this project: HarperCollins, Editorial Vida, Gisella Herazo, the best editor; Itiel Arroyo, thank you for being the connecting bridge; Dr. María del Mar, P. Tito Scarpeta, P. Ariel Muñoz.

I am sure that this book will be an effective tool for winning our battles.

With love
David Scarpeta

CONTENTS

INTRODUCTION

There are terrible things inside of us. Even though we don't show it, we are going a thousand miles an hour inside, fighting battles that, if we could put them up on the screen, would make admirable movies. Often, the same thing happens to us that happens with overloaded pipes. Everything looks normal on the outside, but the moment comes when, due to the pressure we are bearing inside, we burst and the flood gushes out.

I don't know if you can identify with me but, on more than one occasion, I have been astounded to learn of couples who looked wonderful on social media, in church, or at various social events, and then, "unexpectedly," they divorced. At those times, we say incredulously, "But they looked so in love, so committed to each other." Or, we know people who had a solid and healthy spiritual life and "suddenly" fell into adultery or were living a double life. And, going beyond immorality or divorces, we can think of people who looked happy and who, we later learn, were living with horrible depression. The pipe bursts due to the pressure the person is bearing and which *no one was aware of.*

This is the reality. *Everyone* is constantly fighting *internal* battles that are not obvious to other people. These are battles we fight deep inside ourselves, so deeply buried that we do not share them with anyone. Many married people do not even discuss them with their spouses, thinking: "S/he will not understand me," "S/he will judge me," "I will make them worry." What is certain is that there are battles that remain silent on the outside but produce a *real clamor* on the inside.

Think for a moment about the battles you are fighting inside yourself—the ones that are silently draining you, or perhaps even teaching you—the ones that only you and God know about. Then get ready to conquer them, because through this book and the Word of God, you will learn to triumph in your *hidden battles.*

Before beginning this tremendous adventure toward freedom, I would like to remind you that we have been created in the image of God and we are, therefore, people with a mind, soul, thoughts, and will. We are not bodies that carry a soul inside; we are souls contained within a body. One day, this shell called a body will grow old and return to dust, but the soul will go to heaven or hell, depending on in whom we have placed our faith: in Christ for salvation, or in ourselves for perdition. Our internal lives are primarily spiritual, but they deeply affect our emotions, relationships, behavior, and even our health—and therefore our growth as individuals.

You will find the struggles that we all experience in our minds, our emotions, our bodies, and our spirits portrayed in this book, along with the powerful tools given by God to fight and overcome them. Each page and each chapter connects to the next, forming a series of battlefields. In each chapter of this "war record," you will identify an enemy, discover an arsenal equipped with exactly the weapons you need, and find a trench in which to take refuge and to share with someone. You are about to enter not merely a book, but a battlefield that will bear witness to your victory.

Remember that the battle is part of the race of faith that we all run and that there are two groups of people in this race: Those who fight with their human weapons (I am not referring to military weapons, but rather their egos, their knowledge, or their emotions), and those who fight with the spiritual weapons that God gives us. This does not mean they do not have battles, because life is undoubtedly a constant fight; it is about Who is with us in those battles. It is time to decide if we want to be alone, doing what we want or what we think is right, or if we choose to be accompanied by the One who overcomes. His name is *Christ*.

BATTLEFIELDS

My purpose is to help you expand your mind in accordance with the Scriptures. I want you to be aware that we are embroiled in a constant battle. We have enemies, yes, but we also have the weapons needed to triumph and, above all, the Victor is with us.

In this book, we will speak about the different battlefields that lie within you, but before entering these fields, I will give you a road map and a few tools that will serve you on the journey.

What are you going to find?

In each battlefield, you will see three main elements:

- An enemy.
- An armory containing the necessary weapons and plan of action.
- A trench for reflecting, applying what you have learned, and growing in order to move on to the next battlefield.

Let's talk a little about what the trench is. The word trench comes from the Italian term *trincera*, which refers to the ditch soldiers dig in the earth to protect themselves from enemy attacks. In other words, the trench is a *safe place* soldiers build to take shelter and be together. It is very important that you understand this concept, because the spiritual application of this book is developed in a place of trust.

COMRADES IN THE TRENCHES

Do you have friends with the spiritual maturity not to judge you for your vulnerability but instead to understand you and lift you up?

As I told you earlier, more than a motivational work, this book is a *military road map* that will help you to live in complete freedom in Christ. Part of this process is getting to the trench, and there being able to open your heart. Remember: the trench is a safe place.

For this reason, if you have fellow soldiers—companions—find them and enter this battlefield together. Then, when you are in the trenches, you will together be able to do the exercises recommended for growing united in your faith.

Why have comrades in the trenches? Here are a few reasons:

- For accountability. I have learned that accountability leads you to a higher level of responsibility, and that it is not limited to you alone. Accountability has impressive results.
- For the process of healing. When you share your battles with others, you are opening a path to deep and true healing.
- Because you will realize that you are not the only soldier wounded by the same weapon.
- Because you need someone who will set you straight—and then lift you up.

When you read this book with someone who is fighting the same battles as you, you will feel challenged and you will give them permission to encourage you, exhort you, and lift you up. You will allow them to help you shoulder your backpack once more and push you to keep fighting.

Important Clarifications

- Every chapter will include trench exercises, and you will not be able to advance to the next battlefield without first passing through the trench.
- If your trench companions are not in your city or close to you, you can make a virtual trench; however, if you are close to one another, it is better to do the exercises in person.
- There is no limit to the number of trench companions, but my recommendation is that you not form too large a group. Ideally, it should consist of three to six or seven soldiers max.
- If you don't have any soldiers in the trench with you, it is not a problem. Remember that the High Command is at your side: the Trinity—Father, Son, and Holy Spirit.

So pull on your boots and get ready, because we are heading to the battlefield, where your eyes will be opened and you will see what you carry within yourself in a new way. I have prayed that the Lord may open your spiritual eyes so that you may understand through His Word what He has for you, and that you may believe and activate what God has given you to obtain victory in those hidden battles.

Let's go to war!

CHAPTER ONE

SNIPER

Paintball is one game I can't really call my favorite. If you've ever played it, you know you need a stockpile of adrenaline and aggression to spare in order to win.

I have friends who are crazy about this game (they must harbor a frustrated combat soldier inside them), but personally, I don't get much excitement out of it. I've also got to admit that some of my annoyance comes from the fact that, whenever I had to play—because I was invited and couldn't weasel out of it—I ended up with some painful experiences. That's why, if I'm cornered and forced to play, even if I'm dying from the heat, I pile on three more layers of protection than anyone else there. Safety first, you know.

One of the most stressful things about this game, besides paintballs peppering you everywhere, is that you never know where the enemy might be hiding, especially if the game site is in a dark, enclosed area.

I remember when we went out for *paintball* to celebrate one of my sons' birthdays, and he chose a setting with old, abandoned buses. The group consisted of about a dozen or so people, and it was about 9:00 at night (it couldn't get more exciting than this!). We split into two teams, and the fun kicked off for everyone... except me. I'll tell you why: First, I couldn't see a thing; second, my teammates bolted, each to their own hiding place, leaving me alone in an old bus waiting for someone to pass by so I could take them down. Things were looking up when I realized I'd managed to hit several people—until I saw they belonged to my own team. I was definitely on my way to being one of the night's worst players.

What made my experience even worse was the despair and pain of rubber bullets striking every inch of my body when I couldn't tell where they were coming from. I can't tell you how infuriating it all was that all I could feel was the shots against my neck and back. Then I was shooting around crazily, not hitting anyone (except my own teammates, of course). To make matters worse, my opponents noticed my weakness and treated me like a piñata, without mercy. That night I told myself, "I think this is my last time on a *paintball* field."

I'm telling you all this because the same thing happens when we engage in mental and spiritual warfare. Sometimes we are under attack from every side, with no idea where it's coming from or why. We just feel the impact of the bullets meant to destroy us, injuring the most sensitive and unexpected spots.

This is because a sniper is hiding somewhere, waiting for the perfect moment to fire his shots.

WHERE IS THE SNIPER HIDDEN?

I love movies based on real life—and even better if they are action-packed. One of my all-time favorites is *American Sniper.* Bradley Cooper plays the lead role of Chris Kyle, an outstanding Navy SEAL[1] sniper who ranks among the top military snipers of all time. It's said that he recorded more than 255 kills, with 160 officially confirmed during his four tours in the Iraq war.

For those who don't quite understand what a sniper is: He is a military or paramilitary infantryman who is an expert in *concealment* and an elite marksman, shooting with a high-precision rifle over long distances and from *hidden*, places, aiming at specific targets that are carefully selected and calculated down to the millimeter.

Some of the characteristics of a sniper caught my attention while I was watching this movie:

First: the sniper knows where to position himself.

The sniper seeks the most strategic point that allows him a perfect view of his target—obviously without being seen himself.

In the movie, the sniper positions himself on the terraces of houses, behind hanging laundry, and fires his shots from there. The Enemy of our souls does the same thing: He searches for the perfect place and moment, hides, and launches his missiles from his camouflaged position.

I wish to emphasize this: Satan camouflages himself, hiding like the serpent in Genesis 3. The apostle Paul spoke of this in his letter to the Corinthians:

> And no marvel; for Satan himself is transformed [camouflaged] into an angel of light. (2 Corinthians 11:14)

Many people imagine the devil holding a trident, with a long tail and a terrifying face—and, in a sense, this is accurate, since those who have seen demons know their spiritual form is horrifying. But, when the devil gets ready to launch his missiles, he never shows himself as he truly is. He always camouflages himself, waiting for the precise moment, the perfect argument, and the specific bullet with which to attack our minds with deceptive and destructive thoughts that contradict the truth of Christ.

Second: The sniper is very patient. He knows how to wait.

If there is anyone who isn't in a hurry, it's the Enemy. He always knows how to wait in order to attack us at the exact right moment.

> Then was Jesus led up of the Spirit into the wilderness to be tempted of the devil. And *when he had fasted forty days and forty nights*, he was afterward an hungred. And [then] the tempter came. (Matthew 4:1–3, emphasis added)

Satan did not approach Jesus in the Jordan River while the Father affirmed Him, nor did he tempt Him when He was strong in body, nor when He was entering the desert. Satan approached Him when He was hungry. In other words, he waited until Jesus was physically weak in order to "launch his missile." The Enemy knows exactly when to strike.

Third: The sniper is precise—down to the millimeter—in his aim.

Satan does not throw his darts randomly. He knows what he is attacking and is clear in his objective.

It is important for you to understand that the devil's first goal is not to tear down your self-esteem or your dignity. What interests him most is to charge at the truth that God has sown in your heart. What good is healthy self-esteem, sound mental health, or emotional stability if one does not have Christ? Such a person is not the target of the Enemy, because he knows that person is already lost. His focus is on those who have the truth of Christ sown in their hearts. The Lord Jesus Christ told us that the Evil One comes to snatch away what has been sown in the heart (Matthew 13:19).

WE ARE THE TARGET OF A SNIPER WHO IS LAUNCHING HIS EVIL DARTS—NOT ONLY TO DESTROY US BUT ALSO TO TEAR DOWN GOD'S TRUTH IN OUR LIVES.

Fourth: The sniper disappears from the scene once he has completed his mission.

Satan's operational strategy is like that of snipers who move quickly after killing their target. The Enemy is an expert at doing damage, sowing discord, planting the bomb, and then stepping aside. He sets us up to fight among ourselves and then makes us believe that the guilty party in any particular situation is our spouse, our parents, our friends, or our brothers and sisters in the church.

We are the target of a sniper who is launching his evil darts—not only to destroy us, but also to tear down *the truth of God* in our lives. Satan knows that once the truth of God is weakened, we become vulnerable to his lies. That is why, in this battle, his number-one target is our mind—because that is where the truth of God is sown.

Do you know how many thoughts come into your mind each day? According to science, we are capable of generating approximately sixty thousand thoughts daily, of which 95 percent arise automatically, and of those, most are negative. Almost 80 percent of our sixty thousand daily thoughts relate to fear, dread, destructive criticism, sexual temptation, doubt, depression, anger, anxiety, revenge, and many other things. It is astonishing how you can be talking with someone and, at the same time, letting your imagination take flight. For example, when we are in the middle of a meeting and we feel attacked or offended, our mind races a thousand miles an hour, imagining different situations and scenarios—most of them negative. When we witness an injustice that angers us, the mind begins to devise some form of vengeance.

I want you to think about this. How many people have we killed in our minds? How many have we made sick, injured, divorced, imprisoned, or bankrupted? How many thoughts about ourselves have we allowed to drain us and damage not only our self-esteem, but also our identity in Christ? Truly, our mind is a battlefield.

Many of those thoughts are missiles from the Enemy sent for the specific purpose of destroying our faith. The Bible tells us:

> *Above all,* taking the *shield of faith* wherewith ye shall be able to quench all the fiery darts of the wicked. (Ephesians 6:16, emphasis added)

The word the apostle Paul used for "darts" is *belos*, which means "projectile." Obviously, this does not refer to a modern projectile, but rather to an arrow launched from a starting point toward a target. Yet it is not merely a dart, arrow, or projectile—it is set aflame, covered in fire.

Perhaps you have seen war movies set in ancient times in which the burning arrows of the enemy fly everywhere. This is the image that Paul used in this verse. We do not know where these arrows come from or when the enemy's projectiles will arrive in order to destroy the faith that has been planted in our minds.

The sniper is hidden somewhere, launching burning arrows that come from anywhere. Their target is our mind.

I want to reemphasize that, when we speak of the Enemy's burning arrows, we are not only referring to thoughts of sadness, pain, anxiety, vengeance, defeat, or anything else like these. Rather, we are talking about thoughts that go directly against who Christ is and what His work is within us. I say this because, when we speak of cleansing the mind or having a healthy mind, many people focus only on "removing bad thoughts and filling it with good ones." This is not what Scripture tells us. This is not a battle between bad thoughts and good thoughts. We are in a battle between truth and lies—between God's thoughts for us, which are clear in His Word, and the arguments of the devil and our own sinful nature.

God's thoughts are available to us in Scripture.

> For my thoughts are not your thoughts... as the heavens are higher than the earth, so are my ways higher than your ways, and my thoughts than your thoughts. (Isaiah 55:8–9)

In other words, God tells us: "It is impossible for you to have My thoughts. Clearly, you cannot. Just as you cannot reach heaven from earth, you cannot have My thoughts unless you have 'something'." This *something* is described in the following verses.

> For as the rain cometh down, and the snow from heaven, and returneth not thither, but watereth the earth, and maketh it bring forth and bud, that it may give seed to the sower, and bread to the eater: So shall my word be that goeth forth out of my mouth: it shall not return unto me void, but it shall accomplish that which I please, and it shall prosper in the thing whereto I sent it. (Isaiah 55:10–11)

Wow! That is spectacular! God says: "You do not have My thoughts, *but if you receive My Word,* that Word will produce such a powerful change in you that you will know My thoughts through it and *you will have My mind.*" So, when we have the Word of God in our minds and in our hearts, we will have the mind of Christ.

For this reason, the sniper is not merely interested in filling us with "negative" thoughts; *he is interested in preventing us from having the thoughts of God.*

Now, the sniper is exposed! His strategy has always been the same: to refute and cast doubt on the words that come from the mouth of God (see Genesis 3:1, Matthew 4:6), so that they do not produce or complete the work they are meant to do. Jesus illustrated this powerfully in the parable of the sower in Mark 4:15, when He described the sniper's victims as those who hear the Word, but **immediately** Satan comes and steals what has been planted in them.

The sniper's bullets are precise, just as Satan's darts are precise in their intent to destroy us. For this reason, it is important to have sharp discernment, because this will help us find the sniper's hiding place, that is, the spiritual root.

Let's look at the most common darts directed at our minds:

 The Missile of Accusation

> And I heard a loud voice saying in heaven, Now is come salvation, and strength, and the kingdom of our God, and the power of his Christ: for the accuser of our brethren is cast down, which accused them before our God day and night. (Revelation 12:10)

Many people, when they hear the name Satan, are frightened and think of a monster with a tail and horns. But the name literally means, "one who accuses, points out, or seeks to declare another guilty." This is the specialty of the Enemy.

Read me carefully here. The first accusations of Satan against you are not "You're ugly," "Nobody loves you and everyone rejects you," or "You're stupid and worthless." No—the first accusation of Satan relates to cancelling the work of Christ on the cross. "You are guilty and you will not be forgiven." In other words, "The work of the cross and the sacrifice of Christ are not enough to wipe out your evil," He knows that if we believe this lie, every other lie will follow. The culture of accusation is so common today that it has become very easy to accuse one another without fear or reverence for God.

In chapter 3 of the book of Zechariah, the prophet has a vision of the priest Joshua, standing before the angel of the Lord with Satan at his right hand, making accusations. His garments are dirty, but the Lord commands that he be given clean clothing and rebukes Satan, telling him that Joshua was chosen like a brand snatched from the fire. Consider how remarkable this is: What defends us against the missiles of accusation is the truth that, as the children of God, we are chosen to be clean.

The Missile of Doubt

We often think of the devil as he has been depicted to us: a red being with a long tail and a trident. However, the word devil in Greek is *diábolos*, which means "slanderer and accuser." Since the beginning, this Enemy has used the same strategy, employing one of the most effective weapons: doubt.

Think of what happened in the garden of Eden:

> Now the serpent was more subtil than any beast of the field which the Lord God had made. And he said unto the woman, Yea, hath God said, Ye shall not eat of every tree of the garden? (Genesis 3:1)

Satan used the phrase, "hath God said" to address Eve. She responded with the instruction God had given Adam, which Eve knew perfectly. In other words, Satan told her: "God may have given you an instruction, but I have my version." And that is when he wounded her with the missile called doubt, sent by the Enemy to steal the Word of God that had been given to them, as our Lord Jesus Christ said.

> And these are the ones along the path, where the word is sown: when *they* hear, Satan immediately comes and takes away the word that is sown in them. (Mark 4:15 ESV)

This missile is very common, though it is not launched first. Rather, Satan waits until the word is heard and then moves into action to kill or steal this seed. Let me put it this way: If there is doubt about what God has said, it is *proof that He said it.*

The antidote to the missile of doubt is, clearly, the shield of faith. Remember that faith is not a positive attitude. Faith is the spiritual substance that enables us to put our hope in Christ. And, by that faith, we are convinced that God said it and that God will do it. Faith implies fidelity, even in those moments when we can only hear the voice of the Enemy. That is when the faith in which we have believed is tested.

The Missile of Deceit

Let's continue with the sequence of missiles launched at Eve by Satan. After sowing doubt with his question, he went on to deceive her, as written in Genesis 3:4–5:

> And the serpent said unto the woman, Ye shall not surely die: For God doth know that in the day ye eat thereof, then your eyes shall be opened, and ye shall be as gods, knowing good and evil.
>
> The woman was *convinced.*

"You will not die" seemed to be such a powerful and unflinching statement, but it was nothing but a trick. Be careful! Not everything that is said with confidence and firmness is necessarily true. God does not shout, but lies do. Remember that the one sending those missiles is the Father of Lies, because Satan has been lying since the beginning (John 8:44).

THE LESS WE KNOW ABOUT WHAT GOD HAS SAID IN THE SCRIPTURES, THE MORE WE WILL BELIEVE THE LIES OF THE ENEMY.

It is interesting to see the lies that are deceiving this generation, which holds everything that is said to be true. If someone comes along saying that he feels like a woman even though he is a man, and that this is his truth, then everyone must accept and approve of that "truth." There are those who shout absurdities that they insist are truths, but the question is: Are they really true? In many churches, much is preached and little is said, thus fulfilling what Scripture says about the rise of spirits of error and deceit (1 Timothy 4:1). All of these are darts used by the Enemy to deceive us.

I want to make the following clear: Satan's deceit does not merely aim against your identity; he doesn't care what you think. He aims at what God says. I emphasize this because many people limit the lies of the Enemy to the emotional level, relating them to their personal dreams or states of mind (for example, "The devil tells me that I am ugly or that I am not intelligent"). This fact is not to deny that the Enemy uses people to damage our self-esteem, but the deceit of the Enemy goes further than saying that someone is ugly, stupid, or useless. Satan's deceit is focused on contradicting what God has said. This is why the less we know what God has said in the Scriptures, the more we will believe the lies of the Enemy.

The Missile of Pleasure

And when the woman saw that the tree was good for food, and that it was pleasant to the eyes, and a tree to be desired to make one wise, she took of the fruit thereof, and did eat, and gave also unto her husband with her; and he did eat. (Genesis 3:6)

What could be wrong with a fruit if it's so healthy? The point here is that, even though it looked good, it awakened in Eve something that Scripture calls *covetousness.* Covetousness is the desire to obtain something illegally, driven by our natural cravings, in opposition to God's will—and it always leads to pain and destruction.

God loves for us to feel pleasure in those things that He created for us—but pleasure has two sides: one negative and one positive.

On the one hand, think of the delight and pleasure that Adam and Eve experienced in the garden that God created for them (the word *Eden* specifically means "place of delight"). That marvelous garden was full of life; it had crystal-clear rivers—one of which travelled through a region full of gold, according to Genesis

2:10–15—and trees bearing fruit of every flavor and color. Imagine! It was the paradise in which anyone would want to live, with abundance available to enjoy to the full—*except* for the fruit of one tree.

One tree! Just one tree! Amid everything they could enjoy freely, there was only *one* restriction—and it was precisely this forbidden fruit that Eve ate. The missile of pleasure drew her to the delight that the fruit seemed to offer. Doesn't this happen in our lives? There are many beautiful things that God gives us to enjoy and delight in—above all, living in the peace and in the joy we feel when we have a beautiful communion with Him. However, our sinful nature, dragged along by destructive pleasure, leads us toward death.

This dart of pleasure works very well for Satan, because the same thing happens to us that happened with Eve, who, "saw that it was good and delicious to eat," but the end was destruction. Nonetheless, we have the blessing of the Holy Spirit, the Word of God, and our High Priest, the second Adam, who did not sin and who helps us in our weakness.

> For we have not an high priest which cannot be touched with the feeling of our infirmities; but was in all points tempted like as we are, yet without sin. (Hebrews 4:15, emphasis added)

Thousands of years later, the tempter, the ancient serpent (Apocalypse 12:9) came to tempt not Eve and the first Adam, but the last Adam (1 Corinthians 15:45), our Lord Jesus Christ—not in a paradise full of rivers, gold, and fruit, but in a desert (Matthew 4). There, He was also tempted by Satan. In the same way as Satan tempted Eve, although this time without success, the Enemy began to use his strategy, basing it first on the physical need of hunger (Matthew 4:3). Then he attempted to make Him fall into pride, challenging Him to throw Himself off the pinnacle of the temple in the holy city (Matthew 4:5–6), and later transporting him to a high mountain from which he showed Him the kingdoms of the world and their glory, offering them to Him if He would adore him (Matthew 4:8–10). Regardless of the strategy, he failed in every case, because he was confronted with the Word made flesh, our Lord Jesus Christ, who not only knows the Scriptures *but* is the Scripture itself!

Satan relied on pleasure to shoot his darts, but Jesus conquered him with the Word He not only knew but lived.

When the darts come, we must cover ourselves with the shield of faith, which comes from hearing, and hearing comes from the Word of God.

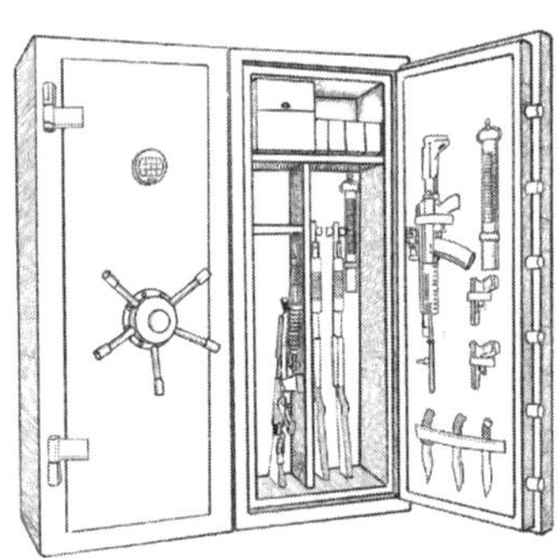

Let's Go to the Armory

As I told you in the beginning, in every battlefield, you will find an armory. Why? Because this book is based on spiritual truths and practices that you can put into action... now!

So let's visit our spiritual armory and get the weapons we need to conquer in this battle.

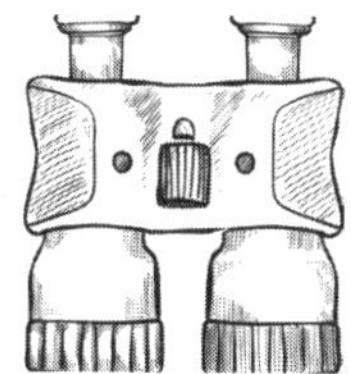

First Weapon: Put on the Binoculars

Have you ever been on a mountain? Have you used binoculars or field glasses to get a better view of the landscape?

When I lived in Colombia, I would go visit a mountain called Monserrate and, at its summit, I liked to use a coin-operated machine with binoculars. When it was first installed, it was a lot of fun—you could see the whole city—but after so much use the view became so blurry that all you could see was the dirty lens.

By contrast, on another occasion I had the opportunity to climb a spectacular mountain, and the friends I was with lent me high-visibility binoculars. Since I was used to the old coin-operated machine, I found it very funny at first: Even with such amazing binoculars, everything looked cloudy. This time, the problem was not the binoculars—it was me. I didn't know how to focus them. Once I learned, the experience was incredible. The vista widened, and I could see details I never would have noticed without that tool. It is fascinating to have such an experience.

Spiritually speaking, God has given us powerful binoculars to be able to see, in the Spirit, what cannot be seen with our natural eyes. These binoculars are called *discernment*.

The Bible urges us to use all means "lest Satan should get an advantage of us: for we are not ignorant of his devices" (2 Corinthians 2:11). What the Lord wishes to tell us through the apostle Paul is that we cannot ignore, avoid, and be blind to the schemes of the devil. The word "scheme" comes from the Greek term *noēma*, which means "thought or meaning." That is to say, we know how the devil thinks and operates. This should not surprise us, because the devil does not create. He copies and repeats what works. He has been this way since the beginning, and he continues to act this way because he gets good results.

For this reason, it is important that we develop the spiritual skill of discernment. Discernment is how those binoculars in the spiritual world show us the arrows and missiles that come from the Enemy toward their target, the mind.

How can we develop spiritual discernment?

The apostle Paul told the Philippians:

> And this I pray, that your love may abound yet more and more in knowledge and in all judgment; *that ye may approve of things that are excellent*; that ye may be sincere and without offence till the day of Christ. (Philippians 1:9–10)

Many people have a false love for God, not a genuine love, because genuine love brings me to know the One I love. To genuinely love God leads us to know Him, and once we are filled with this knowledge, we begin to be transformed into His image. Then we start to read spiritual, and even natural, matters sensibly. That is discernment. The verse says "that you may approve of things that are excellent"—that is, distinguish truth from lies, the good from the bad, and also choose what is best.

When we have the Holy Spirit within us, He will guide us to distinguish what is right. When we have the mind of Christ, we will be able to identify and extinguish the flaming darts of Satan that wish to destroy our faith in Christ. Nonetheless, in order for there to be discernment, there must be a genuine love for God, a transformative love that leads me to know Him more, because it is that love that brings me to the knowledge of God that produces good judgement in me, namely, a right reading of things.

Discernment will help us locate the sniper's hiding place.

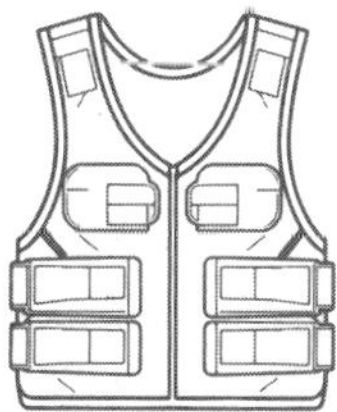

Second Weapon: a Bulletproof Vest

Another of our weapons against the darts of the Enemy is our bulletproof vest—nothing less than the shield of faith.

> Above all, taking the shield of faith, wherewith ye shall be able to quench all the fiery darts of the wicked. (Ephesians 6:16)

I love how this is expressed in the Spanish version of the New Living Translation, using the term levanten—"lift." The original word in Greek that is used here is *analambáno*, which means "to collect, to lift up something that has fallen."

Imagine a warrior whose shield is on the ground while he is under attack from all sides. What is the first thing he will do? Run to get his shield and protect himself. Now, perhaps what comes to mind is a small shield the length of a forearm, one that covers only the upper part of the body—but in those days, shields were not like that. The shield Paul talked about in the original language was called "the great shield" and covered the entire body.

Likewise, it is time to lift up the Word of God that we have allowed to fall in our lives. It is time to take shelter in it and to use it as a shield to stop those arrows—those flaming missiles—of the Enemy.

Remember, the flaming missiles of the Enemy do not come to destroy our self-esteem; they come to destroy the truth and the image of Christ sown within us. Their main goal is to wipe out anything of God in our lives, that is, every word of His sown within us. In this way, he can damage our mind and our vision of God and of ourselves.

In a later chapter, I will teach you some ways to become more effective in the use of the vest and the shield. First, I want to invite you to identify the arrows of the Enemy that have been disturbing your mind, blocking it from retaining God's Word.

Let's Go to the Trenches

You have arrived at the trenches—the safe place to put into practice what you have learned, accompanied by one or more fellow soldiers who walk with you. Now, at the bonfire with your fellow trench companions, do the following exercises with sincerity and transparency.

Let's Sit by the Bonfire

- Write a list of the thoughts—or missiles—that constantly come to your mind. Then, read them aloud (even if you are alone).
- Classify them according to the four types of missiles I told you about earlier: accusation, doubt, deceit, and pleasure.
- Read, reflect, memorize, and talk about these biblical texts, using the weapons you found in the armory:

    - Bulletproof vest against accusations: Romans 8:1.
    - Bulletproof vest against doubt: Numbers 23:19.
    - Bulletproof vest against deceit: John 8:47 and John 10:27.
    - Bulletproof vest against pleasure: Romans 8:13.

- If you have comrades in the trenches, show them this list and ask them to pray for you.

> IMPORTANT: Are you afraid of grenades? You will learn about them in the next chapter—but you will not advance to the next battlefield until you have first passed through the trench.

CHAPTER TWO

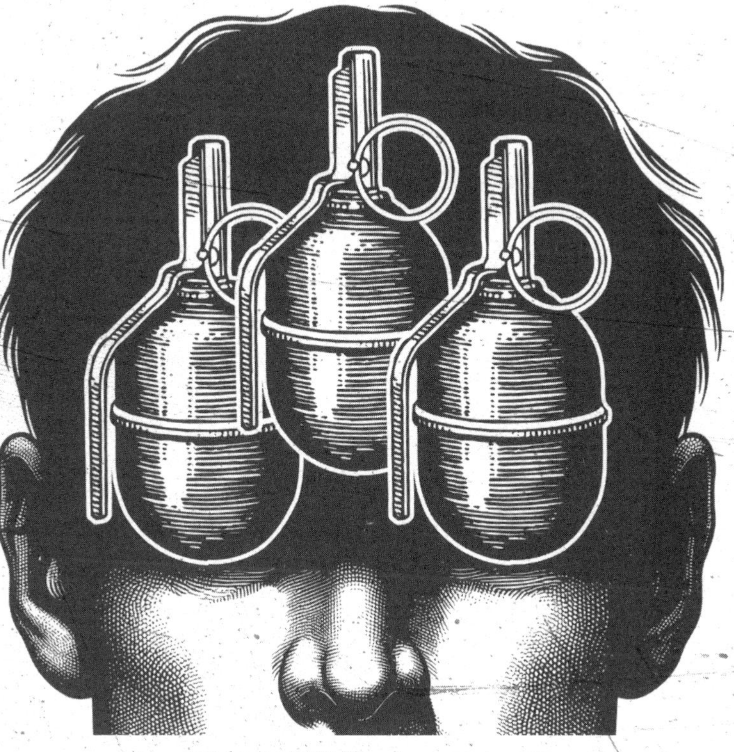

GRENADES IN MY MIND

I think I have already told you that I love action movies, and among those I love most are the ones starring Mark Wahlberg, especially *Mile 22*, which was filmed in Bogotá in 2018.

This movie is about an elite United States intelligence officer who is trying to get a mysterious police officer out of the country. The officer has confidential information, and Wahlberg's character relies on an ultra-secret tactical command unit to help him. Things get complicated when his enemies go to any length to prevent his mission from succeeding, unleashing a dangerous campaign of bullets, missiles, and hand-to-hand combat.

One of my favorite scenes occurs when the officer, James Silva (Mark Wahlberg), and his team find themselves trapped, while one of his key operatives—one of the best elements of the movie—is mortally wounded. She finds herself alone, in agony, knowing that nothing can be done, since very soon her enemies will arrive and finish her off. However, she has something in her hands: two grenades, ready to be detonated, waiting for the aggressors to become the victims. Then, when the enemies arrive, she detonates the grenades and everything around her goes flying. The gory scene ends with flaming cars and bodies destroyed and scattered everywhere.

At this point, I think someone—including my wife, who is always scolding me about this—will say: "Pastor, what are you doing looking at such ugly things?" and my response will be: "I don't know, but I like them." Still, that is not the point (and I doubt this is going to go away, not even with fasting and prayer). The point is that, just as those grenades in the movie have such enormous destructive power, the same thing happens with the grenades that explode in our minds.

I want you to think for a moment about the destruction produced by grenades—the disorder and desolation left behind after they explode. Now consider that the same thing happens in our minds when we let spiritual grenades explode within us.

THE MIND FEEDS ON WHAT WE SEE, WHAT WE HEAR, WHAT WE PERCEIVE, AND WHAT WE SAY.

Allow me to give you a more specific example: You hear something negative that builds a nest in your mind, and instead of putting the pin back in this grenade, you let it explode inside you, causing mental chaos. Now, you can no longer focus—there is a seed of resentment toward someone taking root inside you. You feel unsettled, and you can't even sleep due to the desolation and destruction caused by the explosion.

Later on, we'll look at some grenades that are most common and that build nests in our minds—*with pins removed.* However, before speaking of this, we must take the senses into account, because the mind feeds on what we see, what we hear, what we perceive, and what we say. For now, let's focus on the grenades that come from what we see and what we hear.

What We See

Some grenades are damaging, but others are fatal. I grew up in Bogotá, Colombia, and at that time, narcotics trafficking and ordinary crime were rampant. Robberies, kidnapping, bombs, and terrorist attacks were the order of the day. When I was a teenager, I saw terrible scenes that became engraved in my mind. For example, close to where I lived, they killed the "cocaine queen" and left her bullet-riddled body in front of her house. People simply walked past it, but the impact of what I saw remained etched in my memory. Years later, I found myself in downtown Bogotá when I saw a boy of about sixteen get off of a motorcycle and shoot another man—three times in the head—as he walked down the street. This was another shocking episode, but, thanks to God, neither of these two scenes left my mind traumatized.

Even so, I was once in my living room at home when I saw something that worked its way into my mind and left deep consequences. It was a large grenade that kept exploding over and over again for years, doing me a lot of damage.

I was fourteen years old, watching television in my house one afternoon, when suddenly an image of a naked woman appeared on the screen. I had never seen anything like it—never seen a woman's breasts or her intimate parts—and although it startled me at first, I felt such strong attraction that I continued to watch the television for some time before I turned it off. Just those few minutes were enough for that image to lodge in my mind, along with a chain of grenades without pins that would explode over the following years to come.

That night I went to bed and began to remember the images of the naked woman. I began to feel a sensation that I had never had before, which led me to experience masturbation for the first time.

I know that some people will feel uncomfortable reading this, but it is far more uncomfortable to not speak of it and pretend we were born perfect and free of errors. I want to tell you that part of the purpose of this book is to show that the one writing it has fought very difficult battles—and that these may be the same battles you are facing, the ones no one else knows about. Many people criticize others for addressing difficult subjects, but what they don't admit is that they themselves struggle with these things—sometimes even worse—but they remain silent out of fear. This is why this book exists: *Let's confront those hidden battles.*

Returning to my story, from that time on, I started to masturbate constantly, because I was experiencing feelings I had never had before. That enslaved me for many years, until I found true freedom in Christ. My purpose in sharing this is to help you understand that it all began with a grenade to my mind that entered through my eyes—just as we saw in the previous chapter with Eve and the serpent.

Sexual immorality is fed through the eyes. The power of an image is astonishing, as is the havoc it can wreak. A toxic image can do serious damage that leads to grave consequences. Later, when we go to the armory, we will equip ourselves with powerful weapons that will help us keep a clean mind when faced with killer grenades. And I'm not referring only to those that related to sexual sin, but also to lethal grenades in the form of toxic memories—memories of people who have witnessed the abuse of their mother by their father, drunken rages at home, injustices, deceit, betrayal, and countless other incidents that scar the heart. Even in churches, many have walked away hurt and have not wanted to return because they lived or witnessed situations that were not right.

Perhaps you are one of these people, and if that is the case, I want to tell you that it was not your fault—you were simply there. Other people used and manipulated you, damaging the image you had of certain people and causing deep pain in your life. These are grenades that stayed in your mind, whose pins you pull every time you remember these episodes—and they end up exploding one more time in your head, bringing you back once again to the time and place of the event.

What We Hear

Grenades do not only get into our heads by what we see, but also by what we hear. The following story illustrates this perfectly.

Moses, the great leader of Israel, guided God's people out of the land of Egypt after four hundred years of slavery (Exodus 12:37). God freed the people through Moses with a mighty hand and many extraordinary works—deeds never seen before or since. They then began a journey through the desert they had to cross. The original plan was for this journey to last forty days, at the end of which they would enter their promised land, a land flowing with milk and honey (Exodus 3:17). However, due to the folly and rebellion of the people, what should have lasted forty days turned into a painful journey that lasted forty years (Numbers 32:13).

There is a very interesting episode within this story that became the key reason for that delay—an episode in which an entire generation that had left Egypt with great signs and promises ended up dying in the desert. This story is one of the saddest stories in Israel's history.

> And all the congregation lifted up their voice, and cried; and the people wept that night. And all the children of Israel murmured against Moses and against Aaron: and the whole congregation said unto them, Would God that we had died in the land of Egypt! or would God we had died in this wilderness! And wherefore hath the LORD brought us unto this land, to fall by the sword, that our wives and our children should be a prey? were it not better for us to return into Egypt? (Numbers 14:1–3)

This was the reaction of more than a million people—the number who had come out of Egypt, according to Exodus 12:37, which reports six hundred thousand men on foot, not counting women and children.

Can you imagine more than a million people crying and shouting all night, protesting against Moses? And all for what? A false report they had heard. Moses had sent twelve men to inspect the promised land—all princes of Israel, leaders with authority—among them Caleb and Joshua, who would later become the leader of Israel. These spies went and saw firsthand the nature of the place they were going to conquer. They found a very good land, as God had told them, but it was inhabited by giants they had never seen before.

It is interesting to note that the ten unbelieving spies saw the same things Joshua and Caleb saw, but their report was different, because their mindset was different. Joshua and Caleb had a spiritually superior mindset to those of the others.

Let's consider Caleb's report:

> And Caleb stilled the people before Moses, and said,

> Let us go up at once, and possess it; for we are well able to overcome it. (Numbers 13:30)

This brave man was not putting grenades into the minds of the people, but rather sowing seeds of faith. Even so, the people preferred to listen to and receive the grenades from the other ten spies.

> But the other men that explored the land with him did not agree:
>
> —We cannot go against them! They are stronger than we are!
>
> Then they began *to circulate among the Israelites* the following report about the land: "The land, through which we have gone to search it, is a land that eateth up the inhabitants thereof." (Numbers 13:31–32, emphasis added)

What a grenade they allowed to be planted in their minds—and without a pin! That grenade exploded immediately. They listened to the report, imagined the worst, drew their conclusions, and turned against God and Moses. I call this the "grenade of despair."

Another very common grenade is *gossip*. This one is very powerful, because it acts like a magnet—it draws foolish people, entangles them, and drags them down like an insect trapped in honey. Gossip is like honey for the foolish.

> The words of a talebearer are as wounds, and they go down into the innermost parts of the belly. (Proverbs 18:8)

GOSSIP POISONS US SO DEEPLY THAT IT MAKES US UNTRUSTWORTHY, TOXIC, AND ARROGANT.

Gossip poisons us so deeply that it makes us untrustworthy, toxic, and arrogant; it changes the way we see others, and we even end up speaking ill of people we don't even know. When we pull this grenade out of our mind with our words, we give it the power to explode whenever it wants, causing chaos in ourselves and the people around us with every blast.

We could talk about dozens of grenades that come to damage our minds, but at this point, I think you can identify them. Keep them in mind, because when we go to the armory, we will confront them and disarm them.

SACRED GRENADES

John Calvin said: "The human heart is a perpetual idol factory".[1] We often have grenades in our mind that are "sacred." I'm talking about those thoughts that suddenly cease being threats or enemies and become idols. Wait... I need to tell you again: They were *enemies*, and they became idols! In other words, at first these thoughts were unacceptable, but little by little they gained ground in our minds and now they have their own place, "their throne," so to speak. What's more, we now find these thoughts pleasant and we defend them.

IF YOU HAVE TO SACRIFICE YOUR RELATIONSHIP WITH GOD IN ORDER TO HANG ONTO THEM, THEY ARE "SACRED GRENADES," AND YOU MUST GET THEM OUT OF YOUR MIND AS SOON AS POSSIBLE.

To find out if you have any "sacred grenades" in your life, ask yourself, "Is there anything that used to be nonnegotiable for me that has now become normal to my way of thinking?" For example, damaging habits, worldly culture, or humanistic ideas. To know whether something is a grenade and of no benefit in your life, simply follow this line of reasoning: If you have to sacrifice your relationship with God in order to hang onto it, then it is a "sacred grenade," and you must get it out of your mind as soon as possible.

Now that it's clear which weapon the Enemy uses on this battlefield...

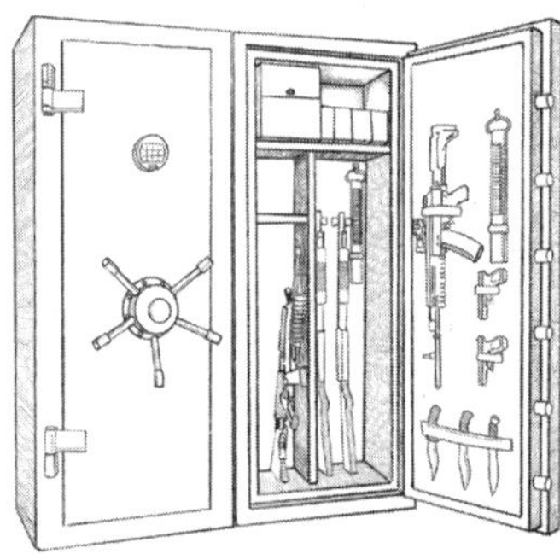

Let's Go to the Armory

Every grenade has a pin in its upper part, held in place by a small lever. Once the pin is removed, the explosion depends on the one holding the lever down. That person has only to stop squeezing the outside lever with their hand and throw it as far as possible for it to explode. They will have no more than five seconds to run and protect themselves.

I'm no weapons expert, but I know enough to translate this to spiritual grenades and the pins we must keep in place in order to keep them from exploding. Let's look at some of them:

The Safety Pin of Submission

The spiritual grenades that want to come and explode in our minds require a pin; that is, we need to learn to submit these thoughts that are contrary to the Word of God and the original plan and hold them captive.

> We demolish arguments and every pretension that sets itself up against the knowledge of God, and we take captive every thought to make it obedient to Christ. (2 Corinthians 10:5, NIV)

The apostle Paul was saying something very powerful here, attempting to make the believers in Corinth see that they had the power to submit every thought that would distract them from the truth of Christ that had been sown in them. The King James Version expresses it this way:

> ...bringing into captivity every thought to the obedience of Christ. (2 Corinthians 10:5)

There are mental grenades intended to destroy the truth within us, but we have the power in Christ to capture them and make them subject to Him. The key is to *submit* contrary thoughts using the spiritual weapons that God has given us, because "we do not war after the flesh" (2 Corinthians 10:3).

THERE ARE MENTAL GRENADES INTENDED TO DESTROY THE TRUTH WITHIN US, BUT WE HAVE THE POWER IN CHRIST TO CAPTURE THEM AND MAKE THEM SUBJECT TO HIM.

Mental grenades that we do not submit to Christ's obedience are dangerous—they are like that grenade without a pin that will destroy everything in no time. Think about it: How many times have you wrestled with mental grenades that you didn't submit to Christ's obedience, and they ended up causing you a lot of harm? It's time to use the spiritual weapons God has given us—to submit these thoughts in prayer and with the power of the Word.

IF YOU ARE SUBMITTED AND ARMED, IT WILL BE THE MIND OF CHRIST THAT WILL RULE YOUR MIND.

Let me give you a practical example: When a grenade with no pin gets into my mind—whether it's a grenade of immorality, abandonment, disbelief, or other thoughts that want to explode—I immediately take it captive in prayer, I bind it and submit it to obedience in Christ. Then, the grenade is deactivated and those thoughts flee.

Now, it's important to clarify that this is not only about submitting our thoughts but also about submitting ourselves—overcoming our sinful nature. Remember this: The more your sinful nature rules your life, the more contrary thoughts will flood your mind. But if you submit and arm yourself, the mind of Christ will rule your mind.

I firmly believe that today, as you read this book, your mind is being transformed—and you will no longer be a slave to these mental grenades. No more chaos!

The Pin of Truth

Just as loins need to be girded, the grenade needs a pin. I love how the apostle Peter related the loins to the mind when he said: "Wherefore gird up the loins of your mind, be sober, and hope to the end for the grace that is to be brought unto you at the revelation of Jesus Christ" (1 Peter 1:13). The apostle Paul also exhorted the Ephesians to stand firm and wear the belt of truth. This is the most necessary protecting safety: *the truth.*

> Stand therefore, having your loins girt about with truth. (Ephesians 6:14)

A PERSON WHO HAS TRAINED HIS MIND WITH THE TRUTH WILL NOT ALLOW GRENADES INTO IT.

A person who has trained his mind with the truth will not allow grenades into it. Think about war movies: When someone throws a grenade at the enemy, the grenade-receiver immediately throws it back? This is the way the system of the truth of the Word works in us. This immune system that defends the truth of Christ in us immediately rises up to throw back and refute any thought that is haughty and disobedient to God.

So, the questions are: How is your belt? Are your mind and your understanding girded? Is the truth sown, affirmed, and rooted in you? If not, the grenades will come, they will nest in your mind, and they will explode mercilessly.

The King James Version expresses it this way:

> "Stand therefore, having your loins girt about with truth." (Ephesians 6:14)

I love the word *defend*, which is used in many Spanish versions of this verse. If you think about it, all of the armor of God that is described in Ephesians 6 is more for defense than attack. There is only one weapon for attack, the sword of the Spirit, which is the Word of God.

IT IS TIME TO SEEK THE TRUTH, LEARN THE TRUTH, BELIEVE IN THE TRUTH, DWELL ON THE TRUTH, AND LIVE THE TRUTH.

The Greek term that this version of the Bible translates as "stand" is *es ístemi*, which means "stand firm and stay that way." In other words, Paul told us: "Stand firm and stay that way, having your loins girt about with truth, and the truth is the very Word of God." Yet we cannot stand on something that we do not believe, we cannot believe in something that we have not learned, and we cannot learn something that we have not sought out. Therefore, it is time to seek the truth, learn the truth, believe the truth, dwell on the truth, and live the truth. This is the key to everything. If I could summarize this entire book in one sentence, it would be the one you just read.

Take heed what you hear

Jesus said: "Take heed what ye hear" (Mark 4:24), and he was not referring to our physical ears but to the ears of the spirit and the mind. When the Word of God enters our ears, it gives us a clear understanding of who Christ is, establishing our identity and opening our understanding to imagine and grow according to His desires and purposes.

How much time do you spend daily listening to and watching things that destroy your mind? What you hear and see shapes the images in your mind, which in turn shape your worldview. Your speech and attitude will inevitably adjust to what your mind absorbs—and that becomes your way of seeing life.

Let's Go to the Trenches

Remember that the trench is a safe place where you, along with your group of soldiers (who should be of the same sex as you), share the experiences had on the battlefield and do the homework before advancing to the next battlefield. If you find yourself alone in the trench, don't worry—the Holy Spirit will be your companion.

Let's Sit by the Bonfire

- Write a list of the music you listen to and of the type of content it expresses.
- Make another list of the shows and series you watch regularly and the type of content they include.

Share and discuss with your comrades in the trenches:

- How much time are you dedicating to reading, studying, and meditating on the Word of God?
- What thoughts do you struggle with most at night?

Choose a passage from Scripture, study it, and meditate on it. Then pray about what God is telling you through this passage. I recommend seeking guidance for this exercise.

- Pray before reading, asking the Holy Spirit to speak to you.
- Look for the following in the biblical passage: a sin to avoid, a command to follow, and a promise to believe.

Important: Do not advance to the next battlefield before going through the trench!

CHAPTER THREE

TARGET PRACTICE

A few years ago, I was shooting with a friend... well, in reality, I was learning how to shoot, since it was the first time I had ever handled a firearm. My friend is a weapons enthusiast, which I am not, and he brought along his entire collection—around ten different types of short- and long-range guns, each with its own ammunition—so I could try them all out. It was quite an experience, *except* for one embarrassing fact: When I tried to hit the target, I hit everything except the target.

My failure to hit the mark caught my attention and made me think. Apart from the obvious fact that I was a novice, I realized there were other factors that influenced my poor aim. For example, I knew what the goal was, but my vision wasn't clear. For example, I knew the point of reference, but I couldn't align my sight properly with the gun.

The same thing happens to many of us. We know what we have to do; we can see it from a distance. Sometimes we even ask for advice or help, and we keep telling ourselves and others, "I know, the target's over there." Yet at the same time, our minds are so clouded that we don't know how to aim and get it right.

The word sin in Hebrew is *kjatá*, and in Greek, *hamartia*. In both cases these mean, "to miss the mark"—in other words, to err. Applied to our spiritual lives, this means to fail, to fall short, to defraud, to commit a crime, or to pervert. The problem is that we generally associate sin only with doing evil—which is true, because sinning is doing evil before God. However, in most cases we don't think about the fact that *not doing good* is also sin.

> Therefore to him that knoweth to do good, and doeth it not, to him it is sin. (James 4:17)

This means that, without knowing it, many of us are sinning not by doing something, but rather by *not* doing something. We're not hitting the target; we are not growing in our spiritual habits; we are not doing the will of God. Instead, we are disconnected from the work of God, focused only on our own needs, not achieving God's purpose for our lives.

WITHOUT KNOWING IT, MANY OF US ARE SINNING NOT BY DOING SOMETHING, BUT RATHER BY *NOT* DOING SOMETHING.

Perhaps we are hitting the target in certain areas—our finances, our studies, losing weight, or completing a project—and that is very good. But the most important target is what we sow in ourselves for eternity. If we are focused on everything except our communion with the Lord, we are simply not hitting the target, because our minds are not aligned with God's purposes.

Many people do not know God's purposes because they do not know His commandments, His instructions, His Word. In other cases, we feel a voice inside us that tells us, "Hey! It's this way!" and we have some idea about where the target is and what we have to do, but our minds are so muddled that we don't move toward the right goal and plan.

WHEN WE BECOME AWARE THAT WE SIN NOT ONLY WHEN WE DO EVIL, BUT ALSO WHEN WE FAIL TO DO GOOD, WE WILL BECOME MORE INTENTIONAL ABOUT PUTTING INTO ACTION WHAT GOD HAS PREPARED FOR US.

Let me to tell you why many people relapse after being restored to Him. The reason is not necessarily that they return to their former ways or destructive habits, but rather that they do not put into practice the works spoken of in Scripture: "For we are his workmanship, created in Christ Jesus unto good works, which God hath before ordained that we should walk in them" (Ephesians 2:10). So, when someone stops doing evil but does not replace it with good, sooner or later that person will revert to their former condition, doing the same things as before—or even worse. When we become aware that we sin not only when we do evil, but also when we fail to do good, we will become more intentional about putting into action what God has prepared for us.

Another reason why I couldn't hit the target when I went shooting with my friend was that my hand was not steady. I could see the goal, but my hand shook when I fired. I didn't have sufficient strength, because my muscles weren't ready to hold up a gun. The image was a funny one, and it made me think, *I'd be better off playing the maracas in a band.*

I remember one of the James Bond movies starring Daniel Craig—my favorite James Bond—in which his arm was badly injured and every time he fired, it was a disaster. However, by practicing over and over, his shooting accuracy returned. The same thing happens when we stop practicing truth and justice, when we stop serving, forgiving, praying, worshiping, and searching the Scriptures. We become habitual sinners, and not necessarily because we are in the sinful world, but rather because we are not focused on the target.

The apostle Peter put it this way:

> And beside this, giving all diligence, add to your faith virtue; and to virtue knowledge; and to knowledge temperance; and to temperance patience; and to patience godliness; and to godliness brotherly kindness; and to brotherly kindness charity. For if these things be in you, and abound, they make you that ye shall neither be barren nor unfruitful in the knowledge of our Lord Jesus Christ. (2 Peter 1:5–8)

How powerful are God's words here! And there are two ways of looking at them. One is to answer, "No way! This is too hard! I feel defeated just reading this." The other way is to see it in the right light. This means understanding that, yes, we must make an effort to grow in faith—but one thing will lead naturally to another: faith leads to goodness, goodness to knowledge, knowledge to self-control, and so on. It is like a magnet that attracts everything. The reason Peter ordered us to do this is because, if we do it, we will not err, we will not be idle, but rather, in contrast, we will be productive and useful. In other words, we will not be like I was—everything but the target.

Sun Tzu, the Chinese general and strategist who lived around the fifth century before Christ, said in one of the war strategy books from his collection: "Armies should only face their rivals when they have a clear battle."[1] Many people fall short in this today. We know we have an enemy, we know what problems burden us and we can count them and define them in words, but we still miss the target, because our minds have not been properly aligned with the Word of God. As Sun Tzu might say, "It is not clear." As long as our mind is lost and clouded, and we don't recognize our battle, it will be very difficult to pick out the target.

The Enemy knows that if our minds are seared closed, attending Christian events, interacting with other believers, or listening to a little worship here and a little more there, will all be good for nothing. As long as our thoughts are programmed according to the world and not according to the military codes of the Scriptures, we will keep wandering in circles—just like Israel in the desert.

LET'S IDENTIFY THE ENEMY

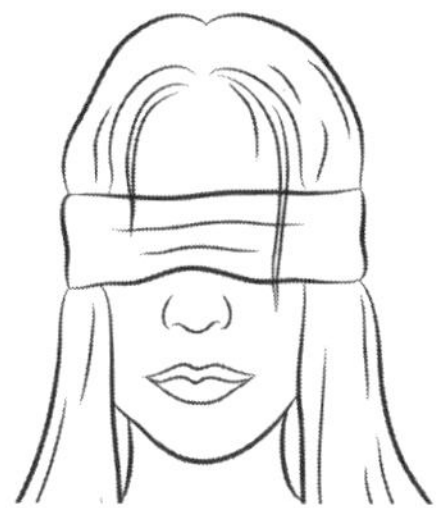

The Hostage's Blindfold

One of the most painful experiences a person can endure is being kidnapped—taken hostage against their will and deprived of freedom in exchange for something. Usually, hostages have their hands tied and are blindfolded so they cannot recognize places or their surroundings.

One of the most striking stories I have read on this subject—and witnessed on the news in my country, Colombia—was the liberation of Ingrid Betancourt, a woman who was a political leader, a former member of the Senate of the Republic of Colombia, and a former presidential candidate.

Ingrid was kidnapped by the FARC guerilla group (Fuerzas Armadas Revolucionarias de Colombia [Revolutionary Armed Forces of Colombia]) on February 23, 2002, during a time when the country was facing a severe political and security crisis under the government of then-president Andrés Pastrana. Pastrana had decided to suspend peace negotiations and reestablish military control over a territorial area previously ceded to the guerrillas. After a press conference, the then-presidential candidate decided to go to the remotest areas of San Vicente del Caguán—an extremely dangerous area dominated by guerrilla forces. Although the government could guarantee her safety, she continued her journey anyway, accompanied by her aide, Clara Rojas. As might have been expected, minutes later, they were kidnapped and taken to the mountains as political hostages.

Ingrid was held hostage for nearly six years, during which she tried unsuccessfully to escape several times. various countries and political leaders attempted interventions, but nothing succeeded in convincing her captors to release her.

The kidnapping of Íngrid Betancourt—one of the most reported on in the history of Colombia—ended on July 2, 2008, when she was freed after a military operation called "Operación Jaque" ("Operation Checkmate"). This is one of the most interesting operations in the Colombian military history, as military intelligence managed to infiltrate the upper ranks of the guerillas, learning their codes and intercepting their communications. Disguised as senior guerilla commanders, the infiltrators gave orders to the kidnappers, instructing them where to take Ingrid. The kidnappers fell for the trick and took her to that specific point, believing they were taking her to their superiors. They didn't know that they were handing over their greatest trophy to the Colombian National Army—and that they were about to be the ones to lose their freedom.

The most moving moment was when they transferred Íngrid, still blindfolded, to the meeting point. Obviously, she did not know where she was, nor where she was going—in contrast to her kidnappers, who knew the area very well—but once the operation was finished and her captors were arrested, they sent her up in a helicopter, took off her blindfold, and told her: "We are the National Army of Colombia. You are free."

There is something deeply important about this story—and it is the reason I share it with you. Just as Íngrid didn't know where she was and was taken captive, this is the reality on the spiritual level for many people: They have been taken captive. Íngrid spent almost six years in captivity, but there are those who spend more time in spiritual and mental captivity because of the blindfolds that cover their understanding. Many of us were held captive for years, blind to spiritural reality and imprisoned in darkness. But, when we came to know the truth of the gospel, our eyes were opened.

On one occasion, when the Lord Jesus Christ entered the synagogue, He was handed the scroll of the Prophets and the Law. Reading from the prophet Isaiah, He said:

> "The Spirit of the Lord is upon me, because he hath anointed me to preach the gospel to the poor; He hath sent me to heal the brokenhearted, to preach deliverance to the

> captives, And *recovering of sight to the blind, to set at liberty them that are bruised"*. (Luke 4:18)

I would like to ask you a few questions. What blindfolds do you have in your mind that are preventing you from seeing what God has planned for you? On what mountain of forgetfulness and captivity do you find yourself? I invite you to identify this blindfold that has been placed over your mind and your heart.

I could say something eloquent at this point, such as, "You need to remove the blindfold of low self-esteem, or the blindfold of negativity, or the blindfold of pessimism, or the blindfold of sadness." But the truth is that that is just nice-sounding rhetoric—and it doesn't really hit the mark.

Let me explain it to you this way: We are all born with a fallen nature and a tendency to stay far from God. And in this sinful nature, our thoughts are programmed without taking God into account. Spiritually speaking, there is a blindfold that darkens our understanding, preventing us from comprehending the things of God. As the apostle Paul said:

> But the natural man receiveth not the things of the Spirit of God: for they are foolishness unto him: neither can he *know* them, because they are spiritually discerned. (1 Corinthians 2:14)

Paul also said:

> In whom the god of this world hath *blinded the minds of them which believe not*, lest the light of the glorious gospel of Christ, who is the image of God, should shine unto them. (2 Corinthians 4:4)

To know God is the greatest knowledge a person can have. In other words, unless the gospel of Christ removes the blindfold from our eyes, we will not be able to either receive or understand the things of God. And the Enemy will be happy to know that his blindfold is working. What I want you to understand by this is that the blindfold that many people need to have removed is the *blindfold of ignorance*—and I am not talking about ignorance related to the economy or culture, but to ignorance about Christ.

To many people, the word *ignorance* is an insult, but let me explain to you what it truly means. The term comes from the Greek *agnoéo*, which means "to not know, to disregard, and to be unaware." In other words, an ignorant person in the eyes of God is not someone primitive or foolish, as we often understand it, but rather someone who does not know, who disregards, someone who has not received revelation.

THE GREATEST IGNORANCE A PERSON CAN HAVE IS TO BE IGNORANT OF GOD.... KNOWING GOD IS THE GREATEST KNOWLEDGE A PERSON CAN HAVE.

However, the greatest ignorance a person can have is to be ignorant of God. It is almost funny to see how many people complain that God ignores them when, in reality, it is we who ignore Him by not wanting to seek Him in order to know Him. Knowing God is the greatest knowledge a person can have. Through the prophet Jeremiah, He said:

> "...but let him that glorieth glory in this, that he understandeth and knoweth me, that I am the Lord." (Jeremiah 9:24)

It is amazing to see how, once we know God, everything falls into place. We don't need to remove one blindfold after another—the blindfold of low self-esteem, of negativity, of pessimism—because when God reveals Himself through His Son, Jesus Christ, *every* blindfold is removed and we can see all things as they really are. Period.

I encourage you to take off the blindfold that has held you captive.

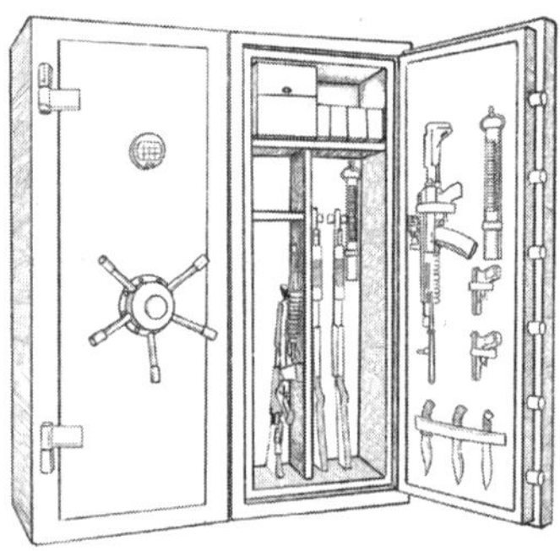

Let's Go to the Armory

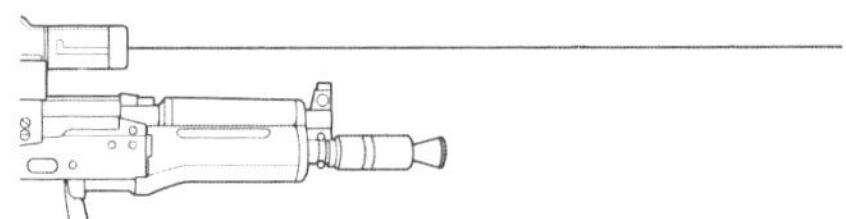

The *Laser Sight*

The *laser sight* is a weapon accessory typically anchored to the eyepiece, which uses a long-range infrared light to indicate the specific point where a soldier must aim, ensuring precision and accuracy in the shot. In our case, that infrared light represents *focus* and *determination.*

BEING FOCUSED IN THIS LIFE IS USELESS IF YOU ARE UNFOCUSED FOR ETERNITY.

Focus is key for hitting the target. But first things first: When we talk about focus, we must center ourselves on the spiritual, because being focused in this life is useless if you are unfocused for eternity. Without the right spiritual perspective, everything else collapses.

FAITH NOT ONLY CONQUERS—IT IS ALSO SACRIFICES.

The author of the Letter to the Hebrews, inspired by the Holy Spirit, told us:

> *Looking unto Jesus the author and finisher of our faith.* (Hebrews 12:2)

To understand this verse, we must first look at its context. Beginning in Chapter 11, the author spoke about what faith is and what it accomplishes, mentioning those who, by faith, achieved incredible things—and others who, by the same faith, suffered cruel persecution. It is essential to understand that faith is not only needed to achieve something, but also to let go and release. It is not only for conquering dreams here on earth, but also for letting them go. It is not only for tearing down walls and closing the mouths of lions, but also for facing the edge of the sword. Faith not only conquers—it also sacrifices.

Thus, after simultaneously giving us such a precise framework and a broad panorama about faith in chapter 11, Paul told us in chapter 12 that it is now our turn to run this race of faith, keeping our eyes fixed on Jesus—whom the New Living Translation calls the champion.

OUR GOAL IS GREATER THAN
A MEDAL OR A DREAM TO ACHIEVE.
OUR GOAL IS CHRIST.

This is not an unreasonable idea, because the author was illustrating a race of faith. In other words, a race that Christ has already won. In the original Greek, the word used in this verse is *arjegós*, which means "ruling leader." The King James Version translates it as "the author," namely, it describes Christ as the prince, he who has authority, the leader of our faith, giving Him not only the descriptor "champion," but also adding much more, since a champion is the one who runs and wins, but is not a ruler. Nonetheless, he who governs is the *master* of the race. And the most impressive part is that Christ, being the master of the race, ran it Himself—demonstrating to us His love and power so that we might follow in His footsteps.

Another fascinating aspect of this text is that Jesus is not just the author, prince, and champion of our faith, but He is also the one who *completes* it. The Greek word used here is *teleiotés*, which is from the same root as the expression Jesus called out from the cross and means "finisher, he who finalizes to perfection." On the cross, Jesus exclaimed: "It is finished, it is done, it is ended. I have the authority. I began and I ended." Therefore, we can conclude that this verse is telling us: "Set your eyes on He who began and completed, on the Champion, on the prince and ruler who has authority." Because of that, even though they may be laudable, our goal is greater than a medal or a dream to achieve. Our goal is Christ.

When our main focus is not *something*, but rather *Someone*, everything else falls into place. In other words, to speak of focus is not merely to know where we are going, but to understand clearly that our goal is Jesus and His purpose for our lives. Paul described it this way:

> Brethren, I count not myself to have apprehended: but this one thing I do, forgetting those things which are behind, and reaching forth unto those things which are before, I press toward the mark for the prize of the high calling of God in Christ Jesus. (Philippians 3:13–14)

What was ahead of Paul? Christ and His calling. To have focus is to fix our attention where we must be. Imagine a soldier about to accomplish the most important mission of his life, with his gaze unblinkingly fixed on the objective. He has only one shot, and it must be accurate. That is the same attitude that we must have every day of our lives: looking at Christ without blinking, without turning our gaze from Him. There are many people who put their focus on themselves. They only see their great achievements and successes, or their internal problems, past or present, nothing else. Yet both fall into the same trap: Both he who condemns himself and he who flatters himself are wrong.

There is an interesting detail in this verse. Paul first says he does only *one* thing, but he later cites *two*. Nonetheless, if we analyze it correctly, those two actions are connected. Forgetting what is behind automatically turns my gaze toward what is ahead; meanwhile, if I continue to look backward, I cannot continue toward the goal. That is, when I do not forget, I am stuck; but when I do forget, I move forward.

DETERMINATION IS A MUSCLE FORGED IN THE MIDST OF OUR BATTLES.

Another weapon becomes available here—one that we cannot buy or acquire in a store, one that is forged within us. As you will remember, I told you that the second reason why my fleeting time as a "cowboy" or "gunslinger" ended in anonymity and disrepute was that my hands could not hold the weapon steady, even less so when it was firing, because they had not been trained for it. Well, this other weapon is associated with our own hands, trained and strengthened to hold the weapon of attack. This is *determination*. Determination is a muscle forged in the midst of our battles.

Speaking of our Champion, Jesus Christ, the author of Hebrews continued saying in the same verse:

> who for the joy that was set before him endured the cross, despising the shame, and is set down at the right hand of the throne of God. (Hebrews 12:2)

Our Champion used these two weapons: *focus* ("for the joy that was set before him") and *determination* ("he endured the cross"). Focus on the goal always gives us the strength to support our weapons and stay in the battle before us.

Today, I pray that your focus will be clarified through this book, that your blindfolds will be removed, that the spiritual vision you are living will be sharp and, above all, that Christ will be revealed to you as the Champion before you.

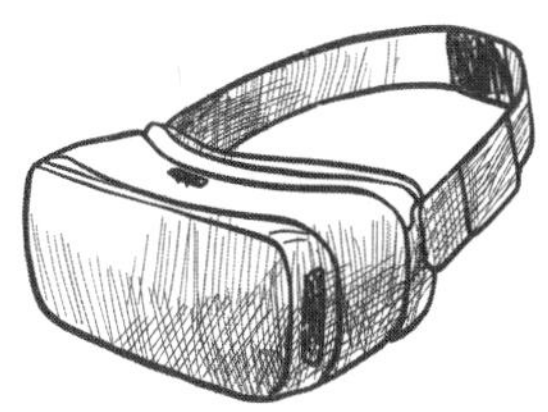

Night-Vision Goggles

The movie *Zero Dark Thirty* portrays the 2011 US military operation that ended in the death of Osama bin Laden. In this operation, following the orders of President Barack Obama, an elite group of twenty-four *Navy SEALs* left in two *Black Hawk* helicopters to a site roughly ninety kilometers from Afghanistan, where their target was located. In only forty minutes—at one o'clock in the morning—they executed their attack and completed their mission, a thing that would have been impossible without night-vision goggles.

If we apply it to what concerns us here, night vision refers to spiritual vision. Here, our night vision goggles have a name: *discernment*. Think about this: How many "operations" have we failed, and how many times have we lost simply because we were not wearing our "night-vision goggles"?

The Greek word for "discernment" is *diákrisis*, which means, "to separate completely, to distinguish and to give a fair opinion." Discernment is that ability given by the Holy Spirit that helps us to see what others do not see—it is those night-vision goggles that help us to distinguish what is from God, what is from us, and what is from Satan. The author of Hebrews wrote the following:

> But strong meat belongeth to them that are of full age, even those who by reason of use have their senses exercised to discern both good and evil. (Hebrews 5:14)

If we base our thoughts on this, we can conclude that discernment is not only a spiritual gift but also a spiritual ability that is acquired through maturity and the exercise of the spiritual disciplines.

Imagine the impressive experience and ability possessed by that group of elite soldiers. The same thing happens with us in our race of faith and in the development of our spiritual maturity. We become people with special discernment—not only through experience, but also through our ability to understand the Scriptures.

I encourage you to examine the condition of your night-vision goggles.

LET'S GO TO THE TRENCHES

Remember that the trench is the safe place where you, together with your group of soldiers (who should be of the same sex as you), share the experiences learned on the battlefield and complete your assignments before moving on to the next battlefield. However, if you are alone in the trench, don't worry—the Holy Spirit is with you.

Here is the guide to the trenches from this battlefield.

Let's Sit by the Bonfire

- Share what moved your heart the most in this chapter.
- Be honest about whether you have been living on the battlefield without focus, and explain why.
- Name the weapons given in this chapter and how capable you are with those weapons.
- Ask your comrades in the trench how each of you can grow more in focusing more on Christ.

Important: Do not move on to the next battlefield before spending time in the trench! See you there!

CHAPTER FOUR

HEARTBREAKING MINES

Some people ask whether I'm Italian because of my last name, and even though it is a last name related to that language (the word *scarpetta* in Italian means, "soak up the pasta sauce on the plate with bread and eat it" and the word scarpa means "shoe"), the truth is that I don't have the least bit of Italian in me—not even the sole of my shoe! The history of the Italian nuances of my last name is very different and, even though I may expose myself to some teasing for telling it, I am going to do so.

My great-great-grandfather lived in the countryside, in the high planes of Cundinamarca, one of Colombia's departments. There were no schools or government entities there, and people were only known by nicknames. He used to dress in several ruanas—wool ponchos—to protect himself from the cold, tying them around his waist with a *cabuya*—a rough rope—as a belt. They said he looked like a folder for holding documents (what we call a "carpeta" in Colombia) and that, for this reason, they called him *Señor Carpeta*, "Mr. Folder." The point is that when a government official came to take a census of the inhabitants of that area, they asked "Mr. Carpeta" for his name and he answered: "Carpeta—but put an S on it; make it Scarpeta."

You might be wondering, *What does all this have to do with mines?* Well, almost nothing—but it's part of my family background, and it helps explain what comes next.

Coming from a family of farmers, my great-grandfather and my grandfather owned potato fields in the countryside, which we used to go visit. Obviously, there were a lot of cows in the there—and that's where my feet first became acquainted with the "souvenirs" cows leave behind in the fields. Perhaps you've had the same experience: Without realizing it, I put my foot—or as they say there, *metí la pata* ("I put my paw")—in cow manure. It's a unique and very disagreeable experience, being in the middle of a field, far from any bathroom or running water, with nothing but grass to wipe your shoes, the cold air biting, the ground damp, the smell impossible to remove until you finally reach a place to clean up. And that's saying nothing about the teasing you get. In short, as I said, it's a miserable experience—but nothing compared to stepping on a real mine.

For more than forty years, Colombia has endured internal war with armed groups. One of the most used weapons in our country has been the antipersonnel mine, commonly called *minas quiebrapatas* ("leg-breaker mines"), which are explosives hidden underground.

Antipersonnel mines are usually used to hinder enemy medical services, degrade the morale of opposing troops, damage unarmored vehicles, and, above all, to seriously wound or mutilate without killing, causing the greatest damage possible, since a dead soldier does not cause as many problems as a wounded one. As such, its most common effects are amputations, mutilations, burns, and lesions of the muscles and internal organs.

Applying this to our spiritual and emotional lives, many of us have been emotionally mutilated, our souls have been crushed, or we have lived through experiences so difficult and shameful that our hearts have been broken. Even though these explosions haven't killed us, we are fighting battles or dealing with the consequences of that "mine" that exploded. And the most difficult thing is that, being wounded and unable to heal completely, we become a burden to those around us.

There is one mine in particular that is devastatingly effective, one that breaks hearts and inflicts deep wounds: *offense*. The word offense comes from the Greek *parάptoma*, which means "false step" (just like when I "put my paw in it" in my grandfather's fields). Therefore, according to the Word of God, an offense is a trap that causes us to make a false step and fall.

Jesus said that stumbling blocks would be inevitable (Luke 17:1), and this is something I want to remind you of: We have all been offended, and we will continue to be offended. For this reason, we have to, on one hand, take care in how we walk and, on the other hand, have a heart that is protected by having practiced forgiveness and having learned to forgive.

There is a person in the Bible who can teach us about this mine of offense, because he was wounded deeply by someone he trusted completely. That person is Philemon.

Philemon was a disciple of the apostle Paul who lived in Colossae, where a church met in his home. He was a man devoted to the work of God and, along with his wife Apphia and his son Archippus, served the Lord. The name Philemon means "friendly," or "one who loves," which gives us a glimpse of his character. I can imagine him receiving everyone who entered his house with love—a man who showed love to everyone.

In this story found in the Scriptures, there are three protagonists: (1) Philemon, the one who was mutilated or hurt; (2) Onesimo, the one who set the heartbreaking mine; and (3) Paul, the soldier who restores. It all began with Onesimo, a man who worked for Philemon as a slave and servant. The slave stole from his master and fled to Rome, where he met Paul, accepted Jesus, and was born again. Paul became his spiritual mentor, forming him as a son in the faith and loving him deeply. Onesimo, fleeing from his problem, found himself with Jesus Christ and made a sincere conversion.

As part of this process, Paul and Onesimo had a conversation about the overdue account that Onesimo had with his former master, Philemon. Let's imagine that conversation:

> Onesimo: Paul, I want to tell you about something—something you may already know. I stole from Philemon when I was his slave, then fled here.
>
> Paul: My dear Onesimo, the reason you arrived here was not to stay with me, but to return to your master. Son, it is time to go back and remedy the damage that you caused. Part of coming to faith is closing the cycles of dishonor that we have created in the past. Remember, God forgives us, but the consequences of our actions are our responsibility. We know that if Christ lives in us, He will give us grace with those people and will use others as means of reconciliation.
>
> Onesimus: But Paul, I don't know if Philemon will take me back, the wrong I did was very serious and could have landed me in prison. If he doesn't forgive me, I will go to jail. It's hard for me, but I'm willing.

> Paul: You will not go back alone, Onesimus. I will send you, and I will be your intercessor and will pray for you.

Paul then wrote this letter to Philemon, saying to him:

> Paul, a prisoner of Jesus Christ, and Timothy our brother, unto Philemon our dearly beloved, and fellow laborer, and to our beloved Apphia, and Archippus our fellowsoldier, and to the church in thy house: Grace to you, and peace, from God our Father and the Lord Jesus Christ.
>
> I thank my God, making mention of thee always in my prayers, hearing of thy love and faith, which thou hast toward the Lord Jesus, and toward all saints; that the communication of thy faith may become effectual by the acknowledging of every good thing which is in you in Christ Jesus. For we have great joy and consolation in thy love, because the bowels of the saints are refreshed by thee, brother. (Philemon 1:1–7)

Paul began by preparing Philemon's heart, because he was about to ask something very difficult of him. Before doing so, he emphasized his virtues—not as a manipulation, but as a loving reminder that he was a man full of compassion, one who had consoled many people. This helps me understand something profound: Offenses are part of the process of our growth.

All of us desire to have a good heart, but there is no way to develop one if the heart has not passed through the heartbreaking minefield. It is there that the heart grows stronger—and most important, where it is tested so that it may become more like the heart of God. This is precisely what Paul wanted Philemon to see. Let's see what he wrote further on:

OFFENSES ARE PART OF THE PROCESS OF OUR GROWTH.

> I ask God, "that the communication of thy faith may become effectual by the acknowledging of every good thing which is in you in Christ Jesus" (Philemon 1:6).

What a tremendous thing Paul told him! "It is time to put things into practice." Let's remember that Philemon was a man with an incredibly noble heart, but even the most noble people need to continue forgiving, even more so forgiving those who have difficult characters.

At some point, all of us will have to put into practice the amens we've spoken, the Word we have learned, the strong and vehement statements we have expressed. And how do we put them into practice? By forgiving the one who planted that mine in our path. Remember, we have all been offended, we are being offended, and we will continue to be offended. There will always be heartbreak mines along the battlefield of faith.

One person once asked Jesus a particularly interesting question about offense—Peter.

> Then came Peter to him, and said,
> "Lord, how oft shall my brother sin against me, and I forgive him? till seven times?"
>
> Jesus saith unto him,
>
> "I say not unto thee, Until seven times: but, Until seventy times seven." (Matthew 18:21–22)

You must forgive over and over again; that is, forever. I imagine Peter keeping a ledger with the names of those who had offended him, asking, "Lord, how many times will I have to forgive those who offends me? In other words, when can I stop forgiving? Because, Lord, I have my limits. I only need to know the law and the right to stop forgiving so that they don't hurt me anymore".

In a certain way, I can understand Peter, because it is normal to set up defense mechanisms against heartbreak mines—that enemy disguised as offense that comes to do so much damage. However, I would like you to think about this: *many times we are offended because we gave place to the offense.* In other words, someone offends us as an act of retaliation for something we ourselves began. For example, it's possible that we were the ones who started the rumor, or spoke wrongly, or spread slander, or did not pay the debt, or did something bad, or did not keep our word. Sometimes we complain about the attitudes of others who come to us in anger without realizing that, in some cases, we were the ones who provoked it.

Now of course, there are heartbreak mines that we neither provoked nor deserved. We did nothing for these things to happen, we were simply going through life and—boom!—stepped on a mine that exploded. This is when we tend to harden our hearts and say: "That's it. I'm done forgiving." We become people with iron hearts—determined never to be hurt again. But in doing so we allow distrust, fear, hatred, resentment, and apathy to take root in our hearts and affect those around us.

NONE OF US WANTS LIMITS ON BLESSING, YET WE PUT LIMITS ON FORGIVENESS.

In both cases, the key lies in Jesus' answer to Peter. "You are always going to have to forgive, because you will be offended many times." We can look at this answer two ways: (1) "Peter, I'm sorry, you will always be affected by the pains in life and by the torture of mistreatment by others toward you," or (2) "Peter, it is better for you to perfect forgiveness in yourself, so that the offenses that may come at any time will not destroy you. Do not put a limit on forgiveness." None of us wants limits on blessing, yet we put limits on forgiveness.

I wish to clarify that when I speak of limits on forgiveness I am not referring to setting boundaries in harmful relationships; rather, I mean placing conditions on whom we choose to forgive. I want to encourage you to consider forgiveness from another perspective: Forgiving makes you more like Christ. He forgave us and gave Himself for us—even in death—while we were still the ones who turned our backs on Him.

Philemon experienced this truth through the offense caused by Onesimo and had to put into practice what he had learned. This brings me to reflect on something: How many times have we asked the Lord to give us a forgiving heart, and He has allowed offenses to come so that this prayer may become reality?

We have already seen the weapon that the enemy uses to mutilate the heart. I now invite you to come with me to the armory to find the *defensive* weapon.

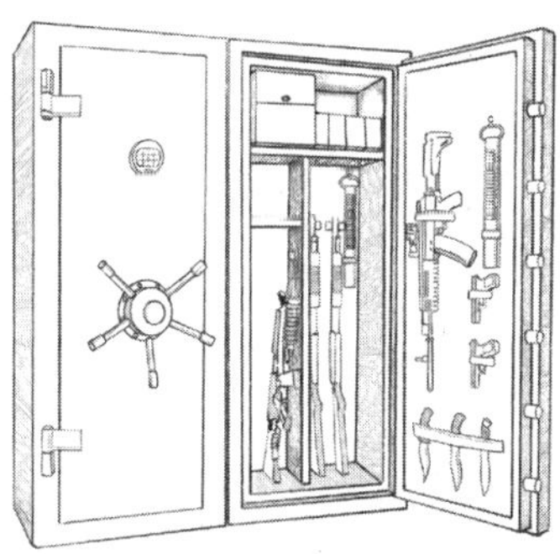

LET'S GO TO THE ARMORY

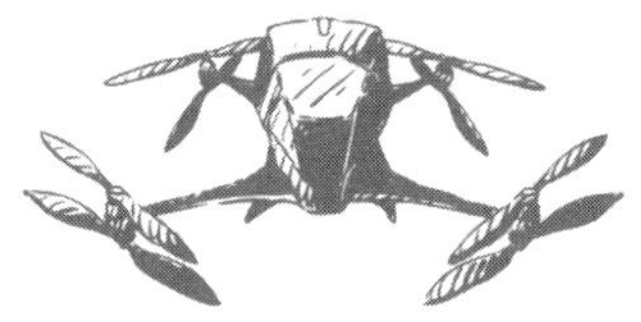

The anti-mine drone

On the night of February 24, 2022, when Russia began the invasion of Ukraine, Igor Klymenko, a seventeen-year-old Ukrainian, was finishing his last year of high school in Kiev, where he lived with his family. The area where they were was becoming more and more dangerous, so he fled to the outskirts to take shelter in a basement with eight other people.

While he was there, the teenager completed his studies remotely and continued perfecting something he had been working on for eight years: his *Quadcopter Mines Detector*—a mine-detecting drone that sends a signal to the operator of the near-exact location of antipersonnel and antivehicle mines. *Clinton Global Initiative*, the foundation of former United States president Bill Clinton, awarded Klymenko one hundred thousand dollars for his remarkable contribution to society.

WE ARE NOT ONLY CALLED TO TURN OUR GAZE TO THINGS ABOVE, BUT ALSO TO SEE THINGS *FROM ABOVE*—AS GOD SEES THEM.

"It was terrifying to hear the airplanes and explosions, but I knew that education was the key to making a difference," said the young man from Edmonton, Canada, where he is studying Mathematics and Computer Sciences at the University of Alberta, one of the nation's five most prestigious universities. "I want to apply what I am learning to develop my drone and solve the worldwide problem of land mines."[1]

A curious detail to highlight here: The anti-mine drone is not a land-based tool—it operates from the air. Establishing an analogy with the spiritual realm, this leads me to think that our calling is not to measure crises or offenses the way those without hope do, but rather as children of God who view everything through a spiritual lens. A spiritually mature person perceives life very differently from someone guided by the flesh or by emotions. We are not only called to turn our gaze to things above, but also to see things *from above*—as God sees them.

What should I do when I find a mine in my path? What do I do when I am offended? There are two key points to remember:

- First, we must learn to deal with offenses. You must remember that the fact that someone commits an offense against you does not mean that you have to be offended. How many offenses, bad words, and unkind comments do we receive from people? I think many, but that doesn't mean that such attitudes have to damage us. Think of it as being offered poisoned food that is set on the table before you. It is *you* who decides whether to eat it or not. Likewise, offense is a plate full of poison set before you. It is a trap in your path, waiting for you in the pit and the void. It is a mine designed to mutilate you—but you can choose not to eat from this plate, not to fall into this trap, not to step on the explosive device.
- Second, we need to take a bird's eye view. When we see things from a drone's perspective, we develop a spiritual view of things. Just as a drone is programmed to detect its targets, our minds remain elevated with a spiritual perspective—programmed with the standards and principles of the Scriptures that have been at work in our lives. Thus, when an offense occurs—that mine, that trap—will meet with a spiritual system planted firmly in our minds, our spirits, and our emotions. That doesn't mean that it won't hurt or affect us, but it is one thing to feel hurt, and another to feel bitter.

When we maintain a daily relationship with the Scriptures—knowing God more and more, talking with Him, and being transformed by His presence—our spiritual vision of things will change and we will be able to discern and identify these mines, thus protecting our hearts from the trap called offense.

OFFENSE IS A PLATE FULL OF POISON SET BEFORE YOU. IT IS A MINE DESIGNED TO MUTILATE YOU—BUT YOU CAN CHOOSE NOT TO EAT FROM THIS PLATE, NOT TO FALL INTO THIS TRAP, NOT TO STEP ON THIS EXPLOSIVE DEVICE.

If you are walking through a season of offense and pain, ask God: "Father, show me what you want to teach me through this moment," and then activate the worldview drone. And if you were to ask me: "David, how do I activate this drone?" I would tell you that first you must understand that the drone is already inside you—you just need to switch it on and update it with the programming of the Scriptures.

When the Word is present in your mind, your thoughts are no longer programmed with what you believe, what the world says, what people post on social media, what unbelieving friends advise, or what you happen to see out there—but by what God says and thinks about the situation.

Here is how the prophet Isaiah expressed it:

> For my thoughts are not your thoughts, neither are your ways my ways, saith the Lord. For as the heavens are higher than the earth, so are my ways higher than your ways, and my thoughts than your thoughts. (Isaiah 55:8–9)

Using our language, it would be saying something like this: "Because my drone is so high up and yours is so low, you cannot see things the way I do." If we stopped reading there, we would be without hope, but because our God is so beautiful, He gives us the key in the following verses:

> "For as the rain cometh down, and the snow from heaven, and returneth not thither, but watereth the earth, and maketh it bring forth and bud, that it may give seed to the sower, and bread to the eater: So shall my word be that goeth forth out of my mouth: it shall not return unto me void, but it shall accomplish that which I please, and it shall prosper in the thing whereto I sent it." (Isaiah 55:10–11)

It is astonishing to know that, even though our thoughts are not the God's thoughts, when His Word falls like rain upon our lives, it lifts us up, enlightens us, and implants His thoughts in our minds and hearts—so that we may have the mind of Christ. In other words, the divine spiritual drone is implanted within us so that we may see, perceive, think, decide, and act according to the ways of God.

If heartbreaking mines explode and we do not have the divine drone programmed into our minds, our decisions will inevitably suffer. But if we activate it—raising our thoughts from the human and carnal to the spiritual and divine—we will not be harmed. The incredible power of God's Word is that it not only aligns our minds but also heals our hearts and makes them grow. Therefore, we will no longer be in a minefield, but in a healthy and protected land.

A Soldier at My Side

When someone has been wounded or crippled by offense, there is no other option but to be carried by fellow soldiers who walk alongside them.

We live in a society where people display perfection on the outside, yet they are deeply wounded on the inside. Especially within the church, we often prefer to hide a wound rather than allow someone to carry us. We've grown accustomed to displaying perfect, error-free lives, hiding the mutilated parts of our soul. However, I have learned the value of vulnerability in my own life.

When we faced the pandemic in 2020, I went through an experience I never imagined I would live through. I went through a very anxious, depressed stage—sleepless nights, days without eating. I prayed and read the Word, but while I was doing so, I sensed the voice of God telling me: *You need to talk with someone.* I was used to fighting my battles alone, convinced I didn't need anyone. But it was at this stage of my life that I realized I needed to embrace the value of accountability. Thank God, the Lord put soldiers at my side who helped me with this difficult process—even though doing so required me to take off my military uniform and reveal my vulnerability.

We need people to lift us up and help us overcome offense. For this reason, I encourage you to read this book with one or two friends in faith so that, together, you can find victory in the internal battles you are fighting.

In the case of Philemon and Onesimo, they were blessed to have the apostle Paul as mediator. Paul acted as intercessor before Philemon—the one who had been offended—and as a protector of Onesimo, the one who had offended.

Throughout our lives, we will often be like Philemon, other times like Onesimo, and still other times like Paul. But in every case, we are perfected in forgiveness. "But David, how will I be perfected in forgiveness?" Well, by forgiving—and more than that, by developing a forgiving heart.

In the story we've been studying, Philemon was perfected by forgiving and taking Onesimo back.

> "For we have great joy and consolation in *thy love*, because the bowels of the saints are *refreshed* by thee, brother." (Philemon 1:7)

The word *refresh* means, "to cause to rest." I think of Philemon as a man who consoled others, and that after forgiving Onesimo, he could minister to and bless the people even more. I can imagine that, when someone came to him saying, "Philemon, look what this person did to me," he could answer, "Remember what Onesimo did to me and how I forgave him?"

Now I would like you to answer this question: Are you someone who sets heartbreak mines to hurt others, or someone who offers refreshment to others? The world is full of people carrying bagfuls of mines—casting them around and wounding many—so we must take care not to be one of them. Philemon's bag wasn't filled with mines but with *oil*—oil that healed and brought peace to others, because true forgiveness includes restitution.

> "Yet for love's sake I rather beseech thee, being such an one as Paul the aged, and now also a prisoner of Jesus Christ."
>
> "I beseech thee for my son Onesimus, whom I have begotten in my bonds: Which in time past was to thee unprofitable, but now profitable to thee and to me: Whom I have sent again: thou therefore receive him, that is, mine own bowels." (Philemon 1:9–12)

The punishment that Onesimo deserved was prison—or even death; Yet Philemon's gift was to restore him to his former position.

What is restoration? To return what a person has lost to them. This applies in two ways: God restores us when we approach Him, but at the same time, He calls on us to restore others. I am not referring to money, but to dignity, worth, and honor. When we forgive others sincerely and bless them, we are restoring them.

Remember, we have all received His grace. Therefore, we can all forgive.

> "I Paul have written it with mine own hand, I will repay it: albeit I do not say to thee how thou owest unto me even thine own self besides." (Philemon 1:19)

LET'S GO TO THE TRENCHES

Remember, the trench is the safe place where you, along with your group of soldiers (who should be of the same sex as you), share the experiences learned on the battlefield and complete your assignments before moving on to the next battlefield. However, if you are alone in the trench, don't worry—the Holy Spirit will always accompany you.

Here is the guide to the trenches from this battlefield.

Let's Sit by the Bonfire

- How are you dealing with offenses? Do you see things from above, like a drone—spiritually—or are you letting your flesh lead you?
- Do you feel offended? By whom, and why? What stage of healing are you in, and what do you need to do next?
- Do you know someone close to you who has been offended by someone else? What are you doing about it?

Important: Do not move on to the next battlefield before going through the trench! See you there!

CHAPTER FIVE

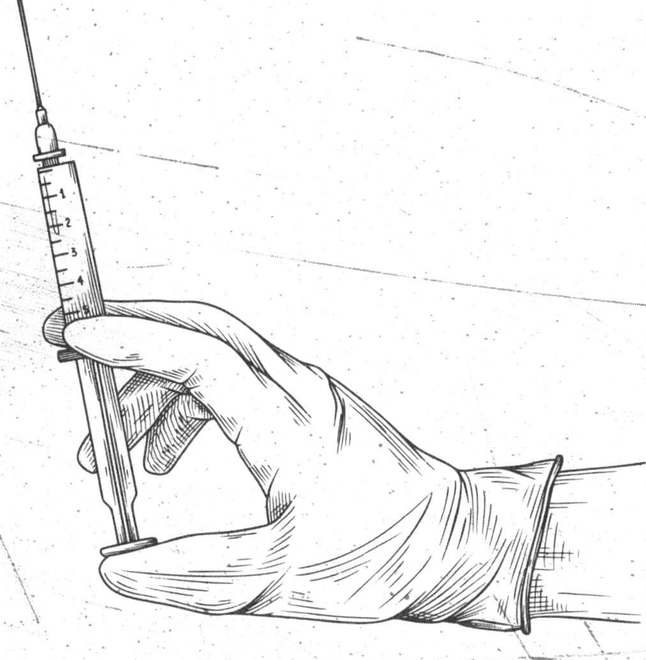

A LETHAL INJECTION

Have you witnessed the power of an injection? Some of them are very effective at revitalizing us if we are weak or our defenses are down. Personally, when I have been traveling, I have had to give myself vitamin injections a number of times, because of physical exhaustion. It's amazing how they help me. So much so that I have chosen to make it a preventive habit.

There are other kinds of injections, though, that don't wake you up—they put you to sleep. Take, for example, the injection given for general anesthesia. These are so powerful that once administered, you become completely unaware of what's happening. In my case, the last time I received one was due to a bladder surgery. I remember that at that moment, the anesthesiologist started talking to be about what would happen while he gave me the injection, but after that, I only remember that I closed my eyes and was completely unconscious. I didn't feel a thing until later, when I had to deal with the pain of recovery when the anesthesia had worn off.

In the spiritual realm, however, there is an injection even more powerful than anesthesia or sedation—a lethal injection designed to silence our cry for freedom, to drain us of the passion to live according to God's purpose for our lives. This lethal injection is called *extreme discouragement*.

A discouraged person is someone without breath, without life, without strength. And a discouraged soldier is an easy target for the enemy.

It's important to mention that no one is safe from discouragement. We have all lived it or experienced it at one time or another. This giant comes relentlessly, not only to attack our souls but to undermine God's purpose for our lives, entering the deepest part of our being with the intent to destroy us—just like a lethal injection. How can we avoid it? Let's look at the example of Elijah, a man with the supernatural support of God, who, from my point of view, is one of the bravest people we find in Scripture.

Elijah often repeated a phrase that had undoubtedly become his truth: "As the Lord God of Israel liveth, before whom I stand" (1 Kings 17:1). Wow—what a powerful declaration! With those words, he was affirming that he lived in the very presence of God, that he heard God clearly, and that God heard Elijah. Yet when Elijah found himself at the peak of his career, after defeating the prophets of Baal and calling down fire from heaven to prove before all Israel that Jehovah is the only true God—he fell into the deepest discouragement of his life. Here is how Scripture describes it:

> But he himself went a day's journey into the wilderness, and came and sat down under a juniper tree: and he requested for himself that he might die; and said, "It is enough; now, O Lord, take away my life; for I am not better than my fathers." (1 Kings 19:4)

How often do we hear people say, "But what happened to so-and-so? He seemed so strong and God used him so much! What happened to him?" That was the case with Elijah.

Elijah was accustomed to seeing the manifestation of the power and the glory of the Lord. He was a man who always had a fresh word from God, who lived in His presence and was the instrument of mighty deeds and miracles. But Elijah was also a man of flesh and bone—and that's a reality we often deny or forget. We are flesh and bone! No matter how anointed we are, we are still imperfect. This was Elijah's reality, who, at that moment, was fleeing from death threats from Jezabel, the wife of the king of Israel. The great prophet, one of the most distinguished figures in the Bible, faced a crisis, perhaps the most dangerous of his life and ministry.

One of the wonderful things about the Bible is that it does not hide the weaknesses and struggles of the people God used. Have you ever thought what it would be like if your name and story were written in the Bible, without filters or concealment? What do you think it would say about you? If the Bible speaks so transparently about the failures and flaws of great men of God, how much more so would it say about us? Certainly, many and worse things than it says about the heroes we find in the Scriptures.

I want to pause here to point out something important: We must be careful and sensible when we refer to the men of God mentioned in the Scriptures. Many people speak lightly, and even preach, about Peter, David, or Moses (to name a few) as if they were the worst and we were perfect. The truth is that they, like us, were fragile and imperfect, but strong in God, through grace alone. And though our specific names are not in the Bible, the stories of the great men and women of God that do appear in the Scriptures make it possible to identify ourselves, so that we may not forget that we continue to be flesh and bone, like them.

Now, returning to Elijah's story, let's look at the root of his discouragement—how this *lethal injection* entered his heart.

There were two people in Elijah's life who represented a problem for him: Ahab, the evil king of Israel, and his wife Jezabel, the most perverse queen who ever existed, whose name represents a spirit that continues to be active today. However, Elijah was confronted with a spiritual battle because there was a spiritual force behind his life and ministry, just as there is behind us. We are absorbed in a constant struggle, just as the Scriptures describe:

> For we wrestle not against flesh and blood, but against principalities, against powers, against the rulers of the darkness of this world, against spiritual wickedness in high places. (Ephesians 6:12)

For this reason, I can confirm that depression will not leave you after a few vacations in Cancún or a trip to Disney World. On the contrary, it is even possible that you will be more depressed when you see the credit card bill you have to pay after the trip. Nor will a few pills cure you, because the root of this is spiritual, emotional, and mental.

How Did Discouragement Get into Elijah's Life, and How Does It Get into Ours?

 After a Great Victory

Elijah had just had an impressive victory in relation to all of Israel. It had not rained for three years because of his word, and then, at his word, the skies opened again. In addition, before all of the people, he called down fire from heaven and slaughtered eight hundred and fifty wizards of Baal.

You might say: "He's made it! That's the peak I would like to reach." Honestly, if someone today called down fire from heaven, people would treat him like a god—who could ever bring him down from there? The prophet of God was at his best. But discouragement arrived immediately afterward.

THE ENEMY OFTEN APPEARS AFTER YOUR GREATEST VICTORY—TO DESTROY YOU.

The Enemy often appears after your greatest victory—to destroy you.

Some time ago, I spoke with a worship leader who was struggling with pornography. He told me that the times when he was most vulnerable were right after a great day in church, where God had moved through him and used him in a powerful way. He told me that he came home thinking: "*I deserve a good rest*"—and that's when temptation would show up on a silver platter. While I was listening to him, I could hear the voice of God telling me: *It doesn't matter to the Enemy how much God can use you. He is always waiting for you when you are alone.*

Even though Elijah's case wasn't one of a hidden sin, it was still related to an enemy lying in wait—behind the curtains.

 Through Words of Invalidation or Intimidation

"Then Jezebel sent a messenger unto Elijah, saying, So let the gods do to me, and more also, if I make not thy life as the life of one of them by tomorrow about this time." (1 Kings 19:2)

Elijah heard the words that Jezebel sent him and gave them shape in a vision. The Bible describes it this way:

> "*And when he saw that*, he arose, and went for his life," (1 Kings 19:3)

It's interesting to note that the gods that Elijah tore down on Mount Carmel are the same ones the witch Jezebel used to threaten him. How often do the giants we've already conquered return to intimidate us—and how easily we let ourselves fall into their trap?

This is why I wish to emphasize the words, seeing. We must take care with how we visualize what we hear. Words are so powerful! At that moment, Elijah did not see Jezabel; he only heard the message she had sent. Yet by hearing that threat, those words created a *vision* in his mind, causing him to see himself with a failed ministry, ending in death.

The same thing happens when we hear some comment or criticism about us and it creates a vision in our minds fueled by fear—a vision on a much larger scale than reality.

Jesus Christ gave us a powerful instruction: "Take heed therefore how ye hear" (Luke 8:18). In other words, pay attention to the way you listen. This is an exercise we must learn to practice daily in our lives, because words create thoughts; thoughts lead to ideas; ideas form conclusions; conclusions generate images; and those fixed images often lead us to make rash and misguided decisions.

At the beginning of my service in the ministry, several leaders wounded me with their words. I most often served as a member of the worship ministry, full of grand dreams and a longing to serve. I remember one time the church bought a new drum set, and I approached my leader and said: "Wow! What a beautiful drum set! Don't you think so?" His answer was: "And what's it to you? Don't be a toad!" For those who do not know, this expression in Colombia (no sea sapo) is used to refer to a person who inserts himself where he does not belong, who has no right to be there, or who is simply a busybody. You can imagine how those words made me feel—small and invalidated. I had recently joined the ministry, and I was hearing these words from not just anyone, but from my leader, a person for whom I had a great deal of respect and admiration. The incident did not make me resent him, but it was very discouraging.

What words of intimidation and invalidation have marked your life negatively? Expressions like: "Why are you doing that?" "You're useless," "You're going to fail," "That's not worth the effort," among many others, are lethal injections to our hearts.

 When We Isolate Ourselves

> And when he saw that, he arose, and went for his life, and came to Beersheba, which belongeth to Judah, and left his servant there. But he himself went a day's journey into the wilderness, and came and sat down under a juniper tree: and he requested for himself that he might die; and said, "It is enough; now, O LORD! take away my life; for I am not better than my fathers." (1 Kings 19:3–4)

This is very important: Elijah was used to walking alone. Remember that it was not until after his crisis that God ordered him to seek out Elisha to prepare him as his successor.

Many people think and teach that God cast Elijah aside by telling him that He was going to anoint Elisha in his place (1 Kings 19:16), but we must not forget that after Elijah called Elisha (1 Kings 19:19) the two traveled together for seven to ten years, and that surely, during that time, Elijah learned how not to be alone.

It is obvious that Elisha did not part from his master, so much so that at the end of Elijah's time here on earth, Elisha told him: "I will not leave you" (2 Kings 2:2), even when Elijah asked him to leave him alone. Elijah, being a powerful man of God, must have learned that walking alone is not good and, what's more, one of the arguments that he had with God was that he had to remain alone.

> "And he said, I have been very jealous for the Lord God of hosts: for the children of Israel have forsaken thy covenant, thrown down thine altars, and slain thy prophets with the sword; and I, even I only, am left; and they seek my life, to take it away." (1 Kings 19:10)

The phrase, "and I, even I only, am left" is the same expression used by many people who become discouraged, and it is exactly where the Enemy wants us, in this place of harmful isolation. In the case of Elijah, there were seven thousand men who had not bent the knee to Baal. That is to say that Elijah was not the only one left; there was a remnant of faithful men like him (1 Kings 19:18). So, it was not that Elijah was alone, it was that he had isolated himself.

LET'S STOP MULTIPLYING THE "JEZABELS" AND START SEEING—AND VALUING—THE SOLDIERS WHO, LIKE US, ARE ALSO FIGHTING THE GOOD FIGHT OF FAITH.

In the movement called *Legendarios* ("Legendaries"), which has blessed many men throughout the world and is led by my friend Chepe Putzu, they have a powerful saying: "Man alone, easy prey." This makes a lot of sense, since when we set ourselves apart and isolate ourselves, we become vulnerable.

Something that I have learned is that, for every "Jezabel" who threatens us, there are many more men and women who love us and take a healthy interest in us. So let's stop multiplying the "Jezabels" and start seeing—and valuing—the soldiers who, like us, are also fighting the good fight of faith.

 When We Feel Disappointed

> And he said, "I have been very jealous for the LORD God of hosts: for the children of Israel have forsaken thy covenant, thrown down thine altars, and slain thy prophets with the sword; and I, even I only, am left; and they seek my life, to take it away." (1 Kings 19:10)

Elijah was disappointed with Israel. After having had no rain for three years because of the sin and disobedience of the people, they still did not return to God (1 Kings 17:1). Then the prophet called all the people to Mount Carmel, restored the altar, and confronted them, saying:

> "How long halt ye between two opinions? if the Lord be God, follow him: but if Baal, then follow him. And the people answered him not a word." (1 Kings 18:21)

Elijah felt frustrated by their indecision and distraction—and by how the kings persecuted and killed the prophets. But he needed to learn that this reality was not in his hands.

That's the point. How often are we frustrated with the bad decisions of others—so much so that we become discouraged, thinking that nothing we do has any effect?

 When We Feel Extreme Exhaustion

Elijah had had a very hard day—physically, spiritually, and emotionally. He was so exhausted that he fell asleep (1 Kings 19:5). He had given all that he had: his strength, his passion, his knowledge, his commitment. But when disappointment and fatigue meet, exhaustion multiplies its power.

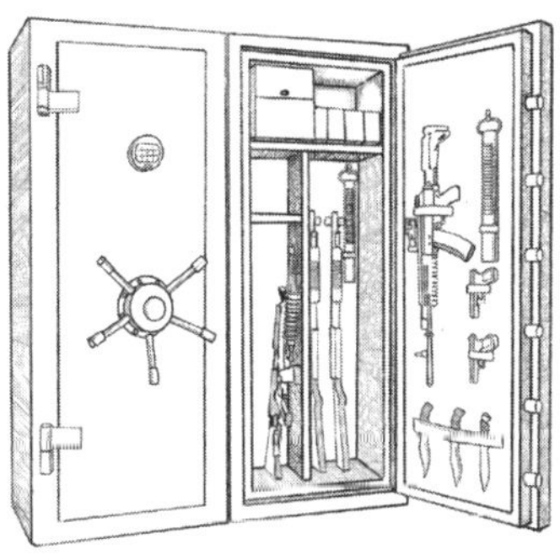

Let's Go to the Armory

In this chapter, we will find two powerful weapons to help us at this difficult stage of our lives. Let's look at the first one.

The Radio Receiver

Every soldier needs a tool that, even though it is not a weapon of attack, can sometimes prove even more vital than a rifle: the radio that keeps the soldier in communication with his central command. This small device has saved the lives of thousands of soldiers. It links central command with the platoon in the field, making it possible for command to come to the rescue. It is a means of communication that keeps them connected with the head of command and makes it possible for them to receive the directions they need to complete the mission. For this reason, the radio operator is one of the most essential people—he carries the backpack with the telephone that enables communication between the soldiers, their comrades, and authorities.

For us, the spiritual radio receiver is communion with our General, that intimate relationship with the Holy Spirit.

Elijah, once a man who lived in the Lord's presence, had begun to hear the voice of Jezabel above the voice of the One who had called him. That's why God himself had to pull him out of the cave where he had put himself in order to teach him an aspect of His voice that Elijah did not know. He showed him a mighty wind, an earthquake, and a blazing fire—but God was not in any of them. God had to re-attune Elijah to His voice.

Let's read how the Scriptures describe it:

> And he said, Go forth, and stand upon the mount before the Lord. And, behold, the Lord passed by, and a great and strong wind rent the mountains, and brake in pieces the rocks before the Lord; but the Lord was not in the wind: and after the wind an earthquake; but the Lord was not in the earthquake: and after the earthquake a fire; but the Lord was not in the fire: and after the fire a still small voice. And it was so, when Elijah heard it, that he wrapped his face in his mantle, and went out, and stood in the entering in of the cave. And, behold, there came a voice unto him, and said, What doest thou here, Elijah? (1 Kings 19:11–13)

Elijah's spiritual radio signal had weakened because of interference—interrupted by the noise of the Jezebel's voice and by Elijah's own, internal voice, which told him: "You're already dead." But God's voice broke though and asked, "What are you doing here?"

What a question! "What are you doing here?" Someone might say, "But, what a silly question! It's obvious—he's in a cave. Don't you see that he is depressed?" But God wasn't looking for answers. He was confronting His servant. Even so, Elijah did not understand Him and, as is the case with human beings, he answered with excuses:

> And he said, I have been very jealous for the Lord God of hosts: because the children of Israel have forsaken thy covenant, thrown down thine altars, and slain thy prophets with the sword; and I, even I only, am left; and they seek my life, to take it away. (1 Kings 19:14)

What's interesting is that God didn't argue with Elijah, nor did He continue His narrative. Instead, He gave a clear instruction, which was a continuation of the words told to him by the angel who brought him food in the desert: "Sit up and eat, because there is a long road ahead of you." Elijah thought that it was all over, but God told him the opposite: "Get up, Elijah, because there is a lot to do, and I am with you." Upon hearing the voice of God so clearly regarding his life, the prophet stopped making excuses and put Jezabel in her place.

Let's restore the signal with central command. Let's reconnect with the Holy Spirit, with His Word, and with our brothers and sisters in faith.

The Recovery Room

This second weapon is not a thing in and of itself, nor is it anything that we ourselves have, but it is something I am passionate about because it is a tool that military bases only use with wounded soldiers.

Every military base has units to care for wounded soldiers, in which the only thing the soldier has to do is to *let himself be cared for* by the staff in charge.

This recovery room is the place where we can see a few things that we did not see before, for example:

He Understands Us

If you and I were God, we might have disqualified Elijah right there. We might have said, "Unbelievable! After everything you've done, now you are here crying and saying stupid things? Why are you asking me to take your life? What is this? You have disappointed me, Elijah!"

Have you thought about how often we become scandalized by our brothers and sisters or friends when they say things in the midst of depression we find shocking? We think, How terrible! I would never say something like that. And yet, God knows us so well and loves us so much that He is patient with us. As the Scripture confirms: "The LORD is merciful and gracious, slow to anger, and plenteous in mercy" (Psalms 103:8).

Though Jesus never fell into depression, He experienced unimaginable pressure in the garden of Gethsemane—a weight no human being could bear. He experienced pain, anquish, and sorrow

> "Then saith he unto them, My soul is exceeding sorrowful, even unto death: tarry ye here, and watch with me." (Matthew 26:38)

This is why Scripture declares that He understands us:

> "For we have not an high priest which cannot be touched with the feeling of our infirmities; but was in all points tempted like *as we are, yet* without sin." (Hebrews 4:15)

The Lord is patient with us in our moments of weakness.

He Sustains Us

> "And as he lay and slept under a juniper tree, behold, then an angel touched him, and said unto him, Arise and eat. And he looked, and, behold, there was a cake baken on the coals, and a cruse of water at his head. And he did eat and drink, and laid him down again... And he arose, and did eat and drink, and went in the strength of that meat forty days and forty nights unto Horeb the mount of God." (1 Kings 19:5–6, 8)

The Lord provided Elijah with His Word and with provisions. He gave him baked bread, warm and recently prepared, using an angel. God still sends messengers today. The Word of God will sustain you. If we are here, it is because He has sustained us in our times of difficulty and discouragement.

> "For I the Lord thy God will hold thy right hand, saying unto thee, Fear not; I will help thee. Fear not, thou worm Jacob, and ye men of Israel; I will help thee, saith the Lord, and thy redeemer, the Holy One of Israel." (Isaiah 41:13–14)

He Finds Us

> "And he arose, and did eat and drink, and went in the strength of that meat forty days and forty nights unto Horeb the mount of God. And he came thither unto a cave, and lodged there;
>
> "and, behold, the word of the LORD came to him,
>
> "and he said unto him, What doest thou here, Elijah?" (1 Kings 19:8–9)

It was not a case of Elijah having lost God—It was that God revealed Himself *right where Elijah was.* The Bible confirms that we can never hide from God.

> Whither shall I go from thy spirit? or whither shall I flee from thy presence? If I ascend up into heaven, thou art there: if I make my bed in hell, behold, thou art there. If I take the wings of the morning, and dwell in the uttermost parts of the sea; Even there shall thy hand lead me, And thy right hand shall hold me. If I say, Surely the darkness shall cover me; Even the night shall be light about me. Yea, the darkness hideth not from thee; but the night shineth as the day: the darkness and the light are both alike to thee. (Psalms 139:7–12)

God called Elijah to serve Him. He supported him at his greatest moment, closed the skies when he asked Him, sustained him during drought, sent fire from the sky when he cried out for it, opened the skies when he ordered it, supported him before every nation, and, in his moment of crisis, depression, and discouragement, never, never, never abandoned him.

God did not just promise to be the beginning and end of your journey. He also promised to be there in the midst of it. He is the God of your whole day. He will come to you in your most difficult moment and find you when no one else can.

GOD DIDN'T PROMISE TO BE WITH YOU ONLY AT THE BEGINNING OR THE END OF YOUR JOURNEY. HE PROMISED ALSO TO BE THERE IN THE MIDDLE OF IT. HE IS THE GOD OF YOUR WHOLE JOURNEY.

How Do We Conquer Depression and Discouragement?

- Don't believe the lies and threats of the Enemy.
- Don't run away. Don't isolate yourself.
- Remember what God has done before—if He did it once, He'll do it again.
- Strengthen yourself with His Word and His Holy Spirit.
- Destroy the spirit of Jezabel, because the battle is spiritual.
- Seek support and practice the principle of accountability.

During the COVID-19 pandemic, I fell into a very deep depression from being closed off, and I sought help. I looked up a friend whom God put in my path and he, with his psychological knowledge and expertise, along with his spiritual maturity, helped me rise again. I thank God for the companions He provides so that we do not walk alone.

To close Elijah's story, it's powerful to see how God ordered this prophet to return to the place where he had suffered shame, but this time to declare victory and judgment.

> "Arise, go down to meet Ahab king of Israel, which is in Samaria: behold, he is in the vineyard of Naboth, whither he is gone down to possess it. And thou shalt speak unto him, saying, Thus saith the Lord, Hast thou killed, and also taken possession? And thou shalt speak unto him, saying, Thus saith the Lord, In the place where dogs licked the blood of Naboth shall dogs lick thy blood, even thine"... And of Jezabel also spake the Lord, saying, "The dogs shall eat Jezebel by the wall of Jezreel." (1 Kings 21:18–19, 23)

God will not let His servants be put to shame! The most beautiful part of this story isn't how Elijah fled and was restored—but how God found him, dealt with him, and restored him. Our God is a champion who will fulfill His plan despite us.

Let's Go to the Trenches

Remember that the trench is the safe place where you, along with your group of soldiers (who should be of the same sex as you) share experiences learned on the battlefield and complete your assignments before moving on to the next battlefield. However, if you are alone in the trench, don't worry—the Holy Spirit is your faithful companion who is always with you.

Here is the guide from the trenches for this battlefield:

- Are you living through a time of discouragement? Why?
- What thoughts arise in your mind when you hear the Enemy's words of intimidation or devaluation? What steps is God showing you today to get out of this moment of discouragement or to be able to deal with discouragement when it comes?

After sharing your answers during your turn, listen to your fellow soldiers and compare your experiences.

Important: Do not move on to the next battlefield before spending time in the trench! See you there!

CHAPTER SIX

BEWARE OF THE HULK!

You may have heard of Dr. Bruce Banner, a socially withdrawn and reserved scientist—physically and emotionally fragile, usually peaceful—who, after accidental exposure to gamma rays during the detonation of an experimental bomb, undergoes a physical transformation into the Hulk (or "the incredible Hulk") when he is subject to intense emotional stress. This often leads to rampages and conflicts that complicate Banner's civilian life. Hulk's level of strength usually corresponds to his level of anger, turning him from a quiet, ordinary man into a green destroyer with a gorilla-sized body. Sound familiar?

This is the image that many of us put forward in our spiritual and emotional life, and that's why in this chapter we're going to take a look at this enemy—an enemy we must learn to master.

We have walked the battlefields of the mind and soul. We have entered the enemy camps called offense and discouragement. Now we need to burst into the camp of this silent enemy, an enemy that could end up controlling us without anyone noticing, because it lurks within us. This is the enemy that feeds jealousy and the cravings that wage war within us—and I'm not referring only to sexual or immoral passions, but to the very thing the apostle Paul spoke of.

> "Now the works of the flesh are manifest, which are these; Adultery, fornication, uncleanness, lasciviousness, idolatry, witchcraft, hatred, variance, emulations, wrath, strife, seditions, heresies, envyings, murders, drunkenness, revellings, and such like: of the which I tell you before, as I have also

> told you in time past, that they which do such things shall not inherit the kingdom of God." (Galatians 5:19–21)

 The Enemy Inside Me

Many people who enlist in the army end up with serious character issues. This condition is defined by the English acronym COSR, which stands for Combat and Operational Stress Reaction.[1]

According to *Military Review*, a professional journal of the United States Army, between 42 percent and 52 percent of soldiers have witnessed episodes of emtional loss of control among their peers due to COSR. Many of these reactions even require clinical care.[2]

I use this example because, although there are important differences between our context and the military context, they do have something in common: the way we react. Many times, our reactions to pressure or to the battles of life are not the most appropriate, because we allow unresolved or uncontrolled areas to affect us—just as many soldiers lose control of themselves under extreme stress. We, as soldiers of Christ, are called to learn how to subdue and control that "Hulk" inside of us.

One of my constant battles is with my temperament. I have a sanguine temperament, and it has led me to make mistakes and rash decisions. Although I consider myself to be a person with charisma, like all sanguine types, I can be very emotional and often lose control. For this reason, I have had to learn to subject every impulse to the dominion of Christ.

I remember one time at the airport, dropping off my wife before a trip. We didn't have much time, which created a lot of stress, and to make matters worse, everything seemed to be working against us. First, we went to the counter to check-in for her flight but, despite the fact that we were the only ones in line, we waited more than ten minutes without anyone helping us. The clock was ticking, and I was feeling more and more stressed out (the Hulk inside me was starting to break out) when I asked one of the airline employees—Admittedly, a bit harshly—to help us.

Then, when it came time to weigh the suitcases, which is a rou tine process when my wife travels, they told us that we had to reduce their weight or pay additional fees. The stress was building, and I was turning green, so I asked my son Natanael to help me take clothing from one suitcase and put it in the other while I continued the check-in process. The problem was that apparently he didn't hear me. When I turned around thinking he had done what I asked, I realized that he had not. And all of this with time running out.

My internal Hulk was getting bigger and was about to come out when, in an angry voice, I told my son: "I asked you to help me with the suitcase! Time is running out and they are going to close the flight!" And for him, a young adult who was also stressed with other things, my scolding didn't sit well and he couldn't think of anything other than to answer me: "Why don't you do it?!" This was when Hulk showed himself and we started to argue in front of everyone there. I want to clarify that Natanael is a very respectful young man and a good son, but the two of us were in a very stressful and tense situation and, although we didn't disrespect each other, we did get angry at each other... or rather, right there in the airport, the Hulk came out of both of us and my wife had to intervene.

Feelings calmed down and we fixed the problem with the suitcases, but we could not avoid the shameful moment when the airline worker, who had witnessed the whole spectacle, gave me my wife's boarding pass and said: "Here are the boarding passes, Pastor David Scarpeta... because you *are* David Scarpeta, right?" I froze when she said these words and answered her: "Well, I think so. Although right now I don't know," to which she answered me: "I listen to your sermons and they have been a great blessing to me." I didn't know what to say other than a brief, "Glory to God," but I was angry at myself inside: "Scarpeta, how embarrassing!" And, as the finishing touch, an old friend was behind us in line, the Christian singer Alex Campos, who, in a spirit of good-natured mockery, said to me: "Beautiful... beautiful!" It was funny and humiliating at the same time. I will never forget that moment when my inner Hulk saw the light.

The Holy Spirit directed James to correct the behavior of believers. And he told us this:

> "From whence come wars and fightings among you? come they not hence, even of your lusts that war in your members?" (James 4:1)

The main idea of his epistle is faith lived out in daily life, confronting the bad attitudes inside us. He spoke about jealousy (James 3:14), false wisdom (James 3:15–17), the tongue that offends (James 3:6), and then continued with the wars and grievances mentioned in James 4:1. The apostle connected the chain of bad behavior with a key question: Where do all these attitudes come from? In other words, Where does that Hulk come from?

The Spanish Word guerra ("war") comes from the Greek *pólemos*, which means "great battles and great uproar." In other words, uproarous war of words, war of arguments. The Spanish word pleitos ("grievances") comes from the Greek *máje*, which means "contensions, fights, discussions." So, in other words, what the

Holy Spirit is asking us through James is, "Where do the battles of arguments, disputes, and fights come from?"

Someone might say: "I know the answer and it is obvious: the stress I have, the problems I face, my problematic spouse that I cannot stand anymore". Someone else might say: "From the injustices I see". And yet another person might say: "I act like this because I have been deeply wounded and I don't trust anyone". Nonetheless, according to the Scriptures, none of this is the root of the problem. The "faithless man or woman" is the symptom. Anger, jealousy, and bad attitudes are only what can be seen. What is the root of it all? James 4:2 tells us clearly: the passions that fight within us.

The word passions comes from the Greek *jedoné*, which means "desires that fight within us," more specifically, "that act as soldiers inside your body." Wow! That means I've got a couple of "Hulks" inside me constantly fighting.

This should lead us to understand that the root of our character conflicts is not the problems we face, but rather the sinful desires that live inside us like an army. The preacher Solomon exhorted us:

> "Be not hasty in thy spirit to be angry: for anger *resteth in the bosom of fools."* (Ecclesiastes 7:9)

The Holy Spirit is telling us through Solomon that anger rests, stays, and belongs to foolish people. Anger doesn't simply show up in fools from time to time and then leave—it *lives* in them. In other words: "Don't disturb the sleeping lion, because he's already there."

NAME IT

This Hulk we've been talking about has a name, and it is not Bruce Banner. It is called rage and anger, and it manifests in a number of ways:

 With cursing

> "...but the tongue can no man tame; it is an unruly evil, full of deadly poison. Therewith bless we God, even the Father; and therewith curse we men, which are made after the similitude of God." (James 3:8–9)

The tongue is the first member of the body that reveals the Hulk inside us, because out of the abundance of the heart the mouth speaks. As I mentioned in the previous chapter, words have impressive power: A sick person will make others sick with his words; an offended person will offend others with his words. And I am not just referring to the fact that we can injure or offend others, but also that we ourselves are often offended. That's when the Hulk gets provoked.

I remember a story from the Scriptures about King David that deeply impacted me. The great king of Israel, a decisive and determined man, confronted one of the hardest moments of his life when he was attacked by his own son, Absolom, who wanted to take the throne from him. Then the king heard some very offensive words from an ordinary person. Here is how the prophet Samuel described it:

> "And thus said Shimei when he cursed, Come out, come out, thou bloody man, and thou man of Belial: the LORD hath returned upon thee all the blood of the house of Saul, in whose stead thou hast reigned; and the LORD hath delivered the kingdom into the hand of Absalom thy son: and,

> behold, thou art taken in thy mischief, because thou art a bloody man.
>
> "Then said Abishai the son of Zeruiah unto the king, Why should this dead dog curse my lord the king? let me go over, I pray thee, and take off his head.
>
> "And the king said, What have I to do with you, ye sons of Zeruiah? so let him curse, because the LORD hath said unto him, Curse David. Who shall then say, Wherefore hast thou done so?" (2 Samuel 16:7–10)

This passage leaves me astonished. David is the king and, in the face of such an offense, any other monarch could have acted with justice or vengeance, even more so when someone he trusted like Abishai was asking permission to kill "this brazen dog." Nonetheless, David's response was incredible, and definitively revealed that he was not the same as he had been years before, as neither his answers nor his reactions were as they had been back then.

The Bible tells us in 1 Samuel 25 that, when David was not yet king and went down with his army, he asked for bread from a foolish man named Nabal, who not only refused to give it to him, but answered his request disrespectfully, saying: "And who is this David that I should give him my bread?" David's reaction in the face of this disrespect was to decide to kill the man along with all of his family. This did not happen due to the intervention of Abigail, Nabal's wife, a woman of good judgment.

I tell you this so that you may take note of an interesting detail: In the case of David and Nabal, the offense was minor, but David's reaction was severe and furious. Nonetheless, in the passage we read before in which David was offended and disrespected as king, and could have ordered the death of the person in question—he answered that his offender should be allowed to live, saying that if God had allowed it, no one could prevent it. Here, David showed us a process of maturity in which he learned to channel the words he heard.

How would we react if someone called us a murderer, a shameless scoundrel, a thief, and said that God would make us pay for everything we had done? Most likely, no matter how Christian we think we are, the Hulk inside of us would rise up "in the name of the Lord." Yet David modeled for us a heart that has learned to keep the Hulk tied up and to walk in humility.

 With schemes and diabolical wisdom

Let's go back to the epistle of James:

> "But if ye have bitter envying and strife in your hearts, glory not, and lie not against the truth. This wisdom descendeth not from above, but is earthly, sensual, devilish." (James 3:14–15)

Anyone can say, "Well, I do not offend anyone. I don't talk like that man talked to David. I don't curse. I don't yell in the house." But the reality is that we probably scheme or mentally replay evil scenarios and nurture unhealthy ambitions. That Hulk named envy and jealousy is very strong—and the anger it produces is very dangerous, because it is an underhanded anger or unwillingness to conform. It eats us up inside, even though we may not show it with transgressions.

 With destructive attitudes

> "Let all bitterness, and wrath, and anger, and clamor, and evil speaking, be put away from you, with all malice." (Ephesians 4:31)

In many cases, the problem is not words, but attitudes, looks, or hate. Today we see so much of this, even in the lives of many believers who simply cannot stand one another. The Hulk is present in these people, and sooner or later, they won't be be able to pretend otherwise or hide it.

The Scriptures warn us: "Be ye angry, and sin not" (Ephesians 4:26). Anger cannot be avoided, but it can be controlled.

Wild, Fragile, and Meek

We encounter three types of people in life: the wild, the fragile, and the meek. The Bible illustrates this beautifully through the lives of three individuals we've likely read about: Moses, the great leader of Israel, and his two siblings, Mary (or Miriam in some biblical versions) and Aaron.

The Scriptures present us with an impressive scene with them in the starring roles, especially Miriam and Aaron. Here is how the episode is described:

> "And Miriam and Aaron spake against Moses because of the Ethiopian woman whom he had married: for he had married an Ethiopian woman. And they said, Hath the Lord indeed spoken only by Moses? hath he not spoken also by us? And the Lord heard it." (Numbers 12:1–2)

This all began because Miriam and Aaron were unhappy with their sister-in-law, the Moses' wife, because she was a Cushite—that is, she was from a non-Jewish race, dark-skinned, and Egyptian. In addition, Miriam thought that she was as capable of speaking for God as her brother Moses, since she said: "Did God only speak through Moses? I am also a prophet." And in fact, maybe her argument made some sense, because it was she who, after crossing the Red Sea, took out her tambourine and prophesied, and in doing so composed a song that we still sing today (Exodus 15). The problem was rooted in the fact that Miriam, as a prophetess and the sister of their greatest leader, allowed the Hulk that resided in her to come out. Then, her critical attitude, along with pride and haughtiness, led her to question the anointing and leadership of Moses—and she convinced her brother Aaron to do the same.

Mary represents the *wild* person, the one who speaks offensively and subtly poisons others. These people have a Hulk disguised as a cat, when in reality they are beasts with claws ready to strike.

The wild person will always look for a fragile person to manipulate and infect with their poison. That is exactly what Miriam did in seeking out her best ally, her brother, the priest Aaron—a *fragile* person who, despite his anointing and assignment, had the serious weakness of letting himself be led around by others. We see this clearly when Moses went up the mountain to be with God and receive the tablets of the Law; while the people below despaired, she spoke to him with arrogance and haughtiness, inciting him to sin (Exodus 32). The result was that he, out of fear of the people, did what they were telling him to do.

MEEKNESS IS NOT A GIFT;
IT IS A FRUIT—AND FRUIT MUST RIPEN.

This also makes me think that the most dangerous people are not the wild ones, but the fragile ones. A few wild individuals can influence many fragile ones, but the fragile ones show themselves to be unstable—those who smile at everyone, but are not on anyone's side. The fragile have no convictions or principles, but allow themselves to be carried away by convenience and influenced by the wild ones.

So then, looking at Moses, Scripture says: "Now the man Moses was very meek, above all the men which were upon the face of the earth." (Numbers 12:3)

The Spanish Word manso ("meek") comes from the Hebrew *anáv*, which means "broken, humble, long-suffering, and submissive," and from the Greek *praus* [TN: this Greek word is also the root of the English, "meek"], meaning "gentle." This was Moses, a long-suffering man, broken and submissive, who learned meekness through brokenness. Let's remember that Moses was an impulsive murderer who lived through some terrible times in his life.

So how did Moses, the man who suffered such terrible crises and lived through such frightening things, later be described as something so beautiful? He came to this because meekness is not a gift; it is a fruit, and fruit must ripen.

So the question we must ask ourselves is, Am I wild, weak or meek? Remember that the subject of this chapter is how to control and tame your Hulk—how to stop being wild or weak so you can become meek. How can we do this? Keep reading.

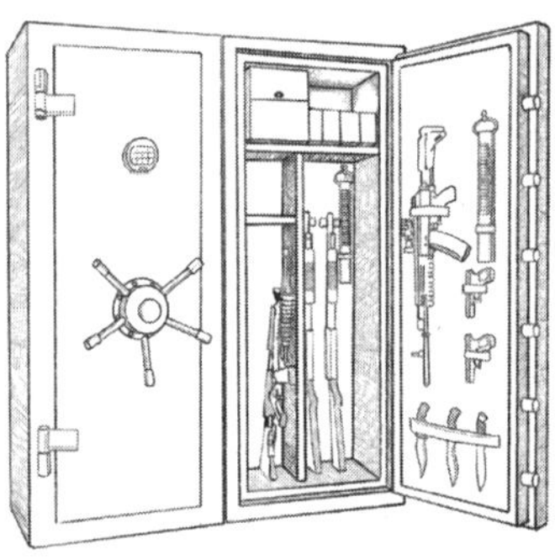

LET'S GO TO THE ARMORY

Care Unit

We've already identified the powerful enemy inside ourselves, but how do we learn to control and subdue it?

In the United States Army, there is a program that offers a very effective treatment developed with advanced technology, which provides specialized care for soldiers with emotional and psychological wounds. This treatment is offered through what is known as the WTU (Warrior Transition Unit[3]). The key to this support process unit cohesion and teamwork; the soldier is not left alone, but walked through the entire process. Many studies have cast light on the fact that the key to emotional restoration for many soldiers is not technological processes, but human companionship.[4]

Applied to ourselves in the spiritual realm, we could call this unit the Warrior Care Unit (WCU).

Our Lord Jesus Christ said something very powerful and beautiful:

> "Come unto me, all ye that labour and are heavy laden, and I will give you rest. Take my yoke upon you, and learn of me; for I am meek and lowly in heart: and ye shall find rest unto your souls. For my yoke is easy, and my burden is light." (Matthew 11:28–30)

Most of us love this promise, but we have to look at the whole context of the conversation, since these words also contain an invitation from Jesus to take up His yoke.

I must confess that I used to think I would give my heaviest burdens to Jesus and He would give me a light one, but that's not how it is. We have to remember that the yoke Jesus refers to is the one placed on a team of oxen—a wooden beam that connects two oxen so that they plough together. We must emphasize that in those times, one of the two oxen was experienced and knew the way and how to plough. For this reason, they put it next to a young and inexperienced ox so that the latter could learn from its companion. I imagine that, at the beginning, it was hard for the young ox to keep the pace, but after walking a while next to the experienced ox, it learned.

The image is beautiful: Jesus already bears the yoke and invites us to walk at His side. He tells us: "Come, walk at my side! I will teach you to be meek and humble of heart, and then your souls will find rest." This truth deeply impacts me because it teaches me that rest does not come from the absence of conflict, but from continually walking with Jesus and being united to Him. That is why Moses was able to do it and set such a powerful example. The key is that he learned to walk with God.

REST DOES NOT COME FROM THE ABSENCE OF CONFLICT, BUT FROM CONTINUALLY WALKING WITH JESUS AND BEING UNITED TO HIM.

Remember, the weapon we are talking about here is the care of the soldier. And who better to care for His brave ones than our God? He cares for us through what we learn as we walk at His side. Our Warrior Care Unit is where we learn to walk in meekness and clothe ourselves in Him.

HOW TO DEFEAT THE HULK?

Put him aside

> Put off concerning the former conversation the old man, which is corrupt according to the deceitful lusts; And be renewed in the spirit of your mind; And that ye put on the new man, which after God is created in righteousness and true holiness.... Be ye angry, and sin not: let not the sun go down upon your wrath: Neither give place to the devil. Let him that stole steal no more: but rather let him labour, working with his hands the thing which is good, that he may have to give to him that needeth. (Ephesians 4:22–24, 26–27)

Here, Paul is speaking to children of God who have the Holy Spirit within them, and the first word in Spanish editions is *desháganse*, which means to put aside or set apart. That said, how do we put the old nature aside?

> "For as many as are led by the Spirit of God, they are the sons of God." (Romans 8:14)

In other words, putting aside the old nature is not a decision that involves self-help or one's own will, based on a power that depends on our humanity. Rather, it is a decision that must be accompanied by the power of the Holy Spirit. Ephesians 4:22 speaks of the "old nature," which is not the one we have now. Now, we have a new nature, so that it is said of us: "You are not the same as before, remember that."

Here are some differences between the old man (dominated by the Hulk) and the new man (dominated by the Spirit of God):

- Hulk allows himself to be dragged around by anger. The new man controls his anger with the help of the Holy Spirit.
- Hulk talks too much and harms others. The new man is wise and edifies others with his words.
- Hulk squanders money. The new man is a wise administrator of the resources he possesses.
- Hulk makes impulsive decisions. The new man seeks the wisdom of God in order to make right decisions.
- Hulk does not have control of himself. The new man exercises the self-control that has been given to him.

It is time to cast aside the old man, who manufactures all deceptive desires and makes us lie to ourselves.

 Build a biblical mind

> In contrast, let the Spirit renew our thoughts and attitudes. (Ephesians 4:23)

The spirit of my mind is the interior life that is reflected in my thoughts and attitudes. The mind is alive and so has a spirit, and the words of Jesus are spirit and life. So, when my mind is programmed with the words of Christ, sooner or later my behavior will follow His principles. This is what it means to have a biblical mind.

 Put on the new man:

> "...and that ye put on the new man, which after God is created in righteousness and true holiness." (Ephesians 4:24)

The word translated here as "put on" is the Greek term *endúo*, which means "to clothe, cover yourself completely like someone who puts a cloak over themselves." The apostle Paul gave us this same exhortation in the letter to the Romans:

> "But put ye on the Lord Jesus Christ." (Romans 13:14)

Before being clothed with my role as father or mother, pastor, student, or spouse, I must be clothed in Jesus Christ, because life is not about being good, but rather about being like Christ. For this reason, we cannot allow space for the devil.

"Be ye angry, and sin not: let not the sun go down upon your wrath: neither give place to the devil." (Ephesians 4:26–27)

The word translated here as "place" is the Greek term *tópos*, which means "opportunity," and the image used is that of a boat during a stay in port. In other words, what God is telling us here is that we must not allow the devil to have a port of entry, much less a port to stay in, in our lives.

Let's Go to the Trenches

Remember that the trench is the safe place where you, along with your group of soldiers—who should be of the same sex as you—share the experiences learned on the battlefield and complete your assignments before going to the next battlefield. Nonetheless, if you find yourself alone in the trench, it is not a problem—the Holy Spirit is with you.

Here is the guide to the trenches for this battlefield:

- How are you reacting to the pressures of life?
- How are you in regard to the subject of anger?
- Share experiences of how you have been harmed by others, but also about how you have harmed others.
- Based on the armory section in this chapter, what weapons do you need to be strong in your lives?

Important: Do not advance to the next battlefield before passing through the trench! See you there!

CHAPTER SEVEN

DON'T LET THE BOMB EXPLODE

In this chapter, we will enter a battlefield of which many are unaware, but on which many soldiers die and many remain stuck in the mud. This is the field where we will fight against our own bodies, namely, with the passions that want to control us.

Many claim the body is not important, arguing that one day it will return to nothing but dust. However, the way in which we use our bodies demonstrates if the Spirit of God really lives within us. That is, if we use our limbs to sin, the one in control inside of us is the old man or the sinful nature, not the Spirit of God. For this reason, it is important to clarify that our body is not only the shell or container where the soul and spirit reside, but also the house where the Holy Spirit lives. Likewise, the body is important because it can be an instrument for our destruction or for our victory.

THE WAY WE USE OUR BODIES DEMONSTRATES IF THE SPIRIT OF GOD REALLY LIVES INSIDE US.

Let me put it this way: our bodies express what is inside us. For example, if there is evil in our hearts, our mouth will speak destruction. If our minds are dirty, our bodies will manifest this mental contamination. If we have bitterness or sadness in our soul, our gaze and our body language will express it sooner or later. And what is worse, our bodies will somatize these unhealthy emotions. For this reason, the apostle Paul reminded us:

> "I beseech you therefore, brethren, by the mercies of God, that ye present your bodies a living sacrifice, holy, acceptable unto God, which is your reasonable service." (Romans 12:1)

Paul urged us to offer our bodies as living sacrifices. So, in this chapter we will talk about sexual purity, and in the next chapter, about caring for our bodily health, since both things make our living sacrifice acceptable to God.

 The Ticking Clock or the Time Bomb

One thing that makes emotions run high is watching a movie scene where a bomb is about to explode. In the scene, the hero has sixty seconds to rescue the prisoners, call the helicopter to take them away, and, while he's at it, kill a hundred enemies waiting for him outside. And the best thing is that, in the movie, he does it! He kills the hundred enemies, rescues the prisoners, and flies off in the helicopter.

This illustration perfectly depicts another of our internal enemies: a bomb with a timer inside ourselves that wishes to control not only our emotions, but also our bodies. This enemy, associated with immoral passions, is called *sinful nature*, which will come to destroy us if we do not stop it.

The Scriptures reference this battle we face:

> "The sinful nature wants to do evil, which is just the opposite of what the Spirit wants. And the Spirit gives us desires *that are the opposite* of what the sinful nature wants. These two forces are constantly fighting each other, so you

> are not free to carry out your good intentions." (Galatians 5:17 NLT)

The term translated as "that are the opposite" is the Greek word *antíkemai*, which means "adversary, opponent." Therefore, the apostle Paul, inspired by the Holy Spirit, showed us a truth in this verse: There is not, nor will there ever be, agreement between the Spirit and the flesh—our sinful nature. There are two adversaries inside us that will never sign a peace agreement, but rather will always be opponents, and as long as we do not understand this, we will be under the conrol of the sinful nature.

In this sense, there are three types of people:

- Those who do not have the Spirit of God within them and live controlled by their sinful nature—without being aware of it. Without the direction of the Holy Spirit, they simply assume, "that's just life"—period.
- Those who are aware of the things of God and the battle inside them. These people know the consequences of living controlled by the flesh, but they are still slaves to it.
- Those who have received the Holy Spirit and have a spiritual awareness of what pleases and does not please the Lord, but also, more importantly, allow themselves to be controlled by the Holy Spirit. As it says in Scripture: "But if ye be led of the Spirit, ye are not under the law" (Galatians 5:18).

James, inspired by the Holy Spirit, spoke to us clearly about the temptation related to this time bomb:

> "Let no man say when he is tempted, I am tempted of God: for *God cannot be tempted* with evil, *neither tempteth he any man*: but every man is tempted, when he is drawn

> away *of his own lust*, and enticed. Then when lust hath conceived, it bringeth forth sin: and sin, when it is finished, bringeth forth death." (James 1:13–15)

This passage clearly tells us that temptation does not come from God, but rather from our own evil desires. In the original text, the image that James used to describe how temptation entices us is that of an animal when it is fooled by bait or a decoy. This is a very accurate description, because just as the animal is dragged away to die, many of us are drawn away, ignoring the time bomb we carry inside, which will destroy us when it explodes.

Let me clarify something here: Temptation is not the same as testing, because testing comes with the purpose of edifying us, but temptation seeks to destroy us.

Now, I want you to pay close attention: Every bomb has a *mechanism*—these days, remotely controlled—that is activated by someone on the outside. In our case, this "someone" is Satan, the tempter (Matthew 4:3), who needs only a *point of contact* inside of us in order to activate a destructive time bomb. That's why, if he succeeds in connecting with an *active bomb* that is ready to explode, the only thing he has to do is push that button called Temptation and... BOOM!

This happened repeatedly to Samson, a man uniquely anointed and gloriously called, but with an active time bomb of sensuality and immorality inside him, which used to explode wherever he went. And that was precisely what led to his downfall. Although he repented at the last minute, his life ended up shattered and his purpose blown to pieces.

Before we continue, I want to ask you some questions. What's going on with this time bomb inside you? Is it active or disarmed?

Is there anything in your life that attracts the tempter and allows him, with just the press of a button, to destroy you? I pray that, as you read the pages of this chapter and step onto this battlefield—where you fight against your own body—you will be open to the power of God and strengthened in your inner being.

 Double Lives

One thing all superheroes have in common—besides having a weak point and a villain who opposes them—is that most of them have a hidden, double identity. When they are not saving the world, they look like ordinary people who live "normal" lives. Thus we can see, among many others, the timid reporter Clark Kent hiding Superman; the millionaire Bruce Wayne hiding Batman; the young Peter Parker, who in reality is Spider-Man; Diana Price, who is Wonder Woman; and the ostentatious Tony Stark, who does not hide that he is Iron Man (my favorite). The curious thing is that while their real identities are very obvious to those of us on the other side of the screen, they are very seldom recognized by the people around them.

Proportionally, something similar happens with us. We have two natures inside us: a renewed nature that seeks to do the will of God, and a sinful nature—the time bomb we are all born with. Let me give you a few examples: It is not necessary to teach a child to not share, because selfishness is in all of us from the time we are little, the tendency to do bad is already present. Likewise, when we commit an error, the sinful nature present in all of us makes us want to hide and cover up the fault. Just as Adam and Eve hid when they sinned, our inclination is to hide when we do something bad.

The same thing happens with lying out of fear of being punished. It's instinctive. No one tells a child, "If you do something wrong, lie and you'll get away with it." Yet automatically the child lies without anyone teaching him. And where does this behavior come from? Who wired up and programmed this time bomb? It comes from our sinful nature.

There are those who think that, even though there is a tendency to do bad, if a person is educated in a family with values, he will change. And yes, this helps. However, no matter how well-educated, ethical, or "good" a person may be, if Christ is not governing his life, at some point he will be taken captive by his sinful nature.

There's a story about a couple eating dinner at a restaurant. They looked very in love and were having a very good time. When dinner ended, they asked to take their leftovers to go, but when they got in their car to leave, they realized that the restaurant cashier had made a mistake. Instead of giving them the bag with food, he had given them the bag with the money that had come into the restaurant that day. In the moment in which the man realized this serious mistake, he immediately went back and returned the bag, saying: "Excuse me, sir, you make a mistake and, instead of giving me my food, you gave me a bag full of money. I cannot go home this way and cause you such terrible harm. Here is your money and, if you would be so kind, could you give me my food. Thank you."

When the cashier saw this act of honesty, he didn't know how to react. The restaurant manager, realizing what had happened, told the man: "Sir, this is the first time I have seen anything like this. How is it that you, having the chance to take the money, came back to give it to us? You are a very honest man, and I would love for this story to go out on the radio, television, and our city's social media. It's a story worth telling. Let me call the news station to interview you, so everyone will know that there are still honest people." Upon hearing these words, the "honest" man answered him: "No, please, don't do that, because the woman I am with is not my wife." This is a reflection of humanity: An apparently honest man of integrity was, at the same time, unfaithful and cheating on his wife.

Today, there are many educated yet sinful people, kind people who are living a double life, people who are very straightforward in their finances or in the order with which they conduct business, but who, at the same time, are controlled by their sinful nature in other aspects. This is why, unless Christ governs our lives, we will not be able to tame this sinful nature—we will not be able to deactivate and disarm this time bomb. However, thanks to God, there is an armory we can go to.

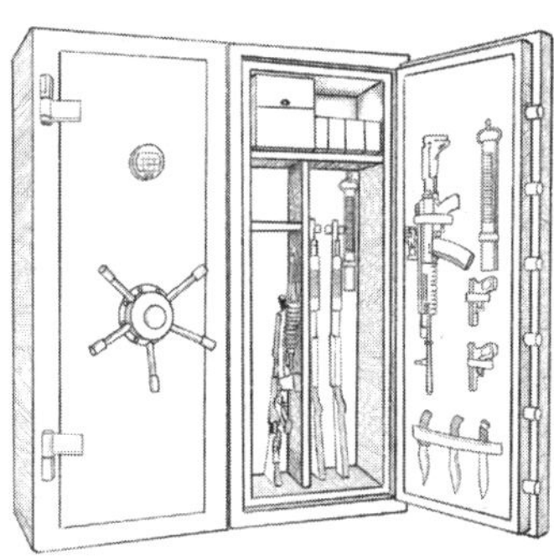

Let's Go to the Armory

TEDAX

TEDAX is an acronym that stands for *Technician Specialist in Deactivation of Explosive Artifacts*. Particularly in Spain, this is the title for those whose job is the neutralization, defusing, and intervention of unauthorized or illegal explosive devices.

When there is an explosive device, an expert who can deactivate it and render it useless is required. And in our lives, this supernatural technician is the Holy Spirit.

God tells us this through the apostle Paul:

> "Therefore, brethren, we are debtors, not to the flesh, to live after the flesh. For if ye live after the flesh, ye shall die: but if ye through the Spirit do mortify the deeds of the body, ye shall live." (Romans 8:12–13)

Here we see three important points:

1. First is what is indicated by the phrase "we are not debtors." Namely, "You do not have to obey your sinful nature. Cease thinking that you are a weak person who always has to do what your sinful nature tells you. You do not have to do it."
2. Second, if we live obeying this sinful nature, we will die. The phrase "live after the flesh" stands out to me. It refers to a way of living to which, sadly, many people are accustomed. They submit themselves to sin all the time. It is not that they fail, it is that they live failure.
3. The third point that Paul gave us is that if we kill the actions of the sinful nature through the Holy Spirit, we will live. Thus, the key here is not to do it by means of our own strength, but rather *with the power of the Spirit.* In words that apply to this book and to this chapter, this is like saying that if you lean on the one who has the power to disactivate this bomb in order to do so, you will not explode into pieces.

Our sinful nature is always there, latent. We cannot escape it until Christ is manifested and comes for us and our bodies are transformed into incorruptible bodies. However, the good news is that the Holy Spirit has the power to deactivate this nature, so that the bomb is inactive and disarmed. And if it wishes to reactivate, the TEDAX will jam it again.

How Can I Strengthen the TEDAX Inside Myself?

Paul, inspired by the Holy Spirit, gave us the answer:

> "There is therefore now no condemnation to them which are in Christ Jesus, who walk not after the flesh, but after the Spirit. For the law of the Spirit of life in Christ Jesus hath made me free from the law of sin and death." (Romans 8:1–2)

The first thing we must consider is that we must be of Christ, since, by belonging to Him, we will not be condemned for our past, present, and future sins. The second thing is that, when we are His, He gives us His Spirit and his power, which restores life to us and frees us from the power of sin. Romans 4 continues this thought:

> "That the righteousness of the law might be fulfilled in us, *who walk not after the flesh*, but after the Spirit." (Romans 8:4)

Namely, this applies to those who, because they belong to God, walk in the path of the Spirit; or rather, they allow themselves *to be governed* by Him. This is the key: to allow oneself to be governed by the Holy Spirit. In this way, when the time bomb that we have within ourselves wants to activate and cause destruction, we can submit these passions to the governance of the Holy Spirit.

Remember this: If you have been born again, the Holy Spirit lives in you and will help you as a unique agent who knows what goes on inside you. He is the one who shapes this inner being, strong and solid, so that, the more you grow in Christ, the less you will allow yourself to be dominated by and subject to your sinful nature.

Let me illustrate this with an example. One of my favorite heroes from science fiction is Iron Man. In one of his first movies, they show his origin as a superhero: While in the Middle East he is mortally wounded and undergoes an inventive process that turns him into a human with unique abilities. That's when he wakes up with a new "heart"—a device in his chest from which he gets all his energy and power. He ends up being a human with superpowers who remains weak unless he uses his superhero suit. Only then can he perform extraordinary feats.

Every time this character returns from a mission—even when he comes back badly damaged—he immediately focuses on operating on himself, reinforcing his weaponry, and improving his modern metallic system so that he will prevail in the next mission. If he had not focused on perfecting his system and mechanisms, he would not have been able to complete the missions he did.

The same thing happens with us. If we focus only on nurturing our flesh and connecting more and more wires to the time bomb that is our sinful nature, instead of strengthening and improving our relationship with God, we will never allow this inner man to grow. Here is how the apostle Paul put it for us:

> "For which cause we faint not; but though our outward man perish, yet the inward man is renewed day by day." (2 Corinthians 4:16)

The Spirit of God is the One who implants the inner man in us. Our spirit, enlivened and strengthened by the Spirit of God in us, is this "Iron Man" who needs to be cultivated and strengthened so that the old man—who, as old as he might be, does not want to die—can be subjected to the new system of spiritual programming that makes us stronger and turns us into conquerors in Christ.

Disarm the Bomb

Before heading to the trenches, I will give you some more tools for disarming this time bomb called *immoral passions.*

One of the most difficult areas to submit to God is our sexuality. It is not a secret to anyone that many, many of us fight intense and silent, internal battles in this area—yet these are the battles that we hide the most. For example, it is easy to own up to it when we feel discouraged or sad. It's normal in a group of friends to ask for prayer when we are sick, or because we feel overwhelmed with problems, family situations, or economic difficulties. Nonetheless, it is not common for someone to say, "Pray for me because I'm committing adultery," or "I'm sleeping with my girlfriend," or "I'm looking at pornography every night." This is not normal, because these sins are hidden. For this reason, my intention with this book is to give you tools to obtain victory in these secret battles that you are fighting. And this area of sexuality is key for your integral development and growth, as well as for you to be able to attain God's promises for your life.

To help you in a practical way, let's look at some things that negatively influence the area of sexuality, considering why and how we fall, and how to pick ourselves up again. Remember that if we are subject to the nature of God in Christ, we will be able to see every aspect of this list from the correct perspective. Let's begin:

 Solitude

How we spend our time alone is key to both our development and our destruction. I will show you two examples of people who spent their alone time differently: one, allowing himself to be driven by his passions; and the other in a correct way, subjected to the divine nature.

HOW WE SPEND OUR TIME ALONE IS KEY—BOTH FOR OUR DEVELOPMENT AND FOR OUR DESTRUCTION.

Let's Look at the First Example: The Case of David

> And it came to pass, after the year was expired, at the time when kings go forth to battle, that David sent Joab, and his servants with him, and all Israel; and they destroyed the children of Ammon, and besieged Rabbah. But David tarried still at Jerusalem. (2 Samuel 11:1)

In fact, David was at a moment in his life in which he had conquered cities and achieved almost everything. However, as the Scriptures say: "He that is slow to anger is better than the mighty; and he that ruleth his spirit than he that taketh a city" (Proverbs 16:32). He was a dynamic man, talented in war, accustomed to combat since his youth—fierce, agile, responsible. Nonetheless, as the years passed, he had entered "relax mode." It is interesting that the text says that is was the time when *kings go forth to battle*, which is to say that David, as king, had the responsibility to go to battle, but he decided to stay alone in his palace.

I want to emphasize that two factors come together here: idleness and the lack of responsibility. And I emphasize this because, when a person ceases to be responsible, focused, and productive—sleeping in the berth of comfort and the bed of idleness—his fall is about to happen. If someone falls into pornography, he doesn't do it energetically, but rather seeking and seeing calmly, letting the minutes and hours pass, and there, in that bed of idleness, the fall begins.

WHEN A PERSON CEASES TO BE RESPONSIBLE, FOCUSED, AND PRODUCTIVE, SLEEPING IN THE BERTH OF COMFORT AND THE BED OF IDLENESS, HIS FALL IS ABOUT TO HAPPEN.

However, pay attention to this: Idleness arises from within—but so does responsibility. Idleness and responsibility both develop in solitude. In other words, he who is focused and responsible takes care of his interior life and uses his moments of solitude productively, even when he is resting.

For many people, it is hard to be alone, because they have not made solitude an ally for growth, but a hiding place—like a cave for sin or depression. But let me tell you something: Solitude is not bad. What is bad are the destructive habits we practice in our solitude. Your failure or success is determined by what happens in your solitude. For example, this book is the result of a responsible moment in my solitude. You are reading it today because I chose productivity and responsibility over idleness.

David sent his generals to fight while he stayed alone in his bed of idleness. I imagine him thinking, *I'm not going to war today. I have already fought many battles, conquered many kingdoms, and subjected many kings. I deserve a rest.* And it is true that we deserve rest! That is not the problem. The problem arises when we distance ourselves from God and these breaks, instead of becoming opportunities to rest in Him, become an escape for our own destruction.

SOLITUDE IS NOT BAD. WHAT IS BAD ARE THE DESTRUCTIVE HABITS WE PRACTICE IN OUR SOLITUDE. YOUR FAILURE OR SUCCESS ARE DETERMINED BY WHAT HAPPENS IN YOUR SOLITUDE.

And so David began walking around his royal palace and, in his solitude, found himself attracted to a beautiful woman named Bathsheba. Many of us already know the story and what happened after, but if you don't know it, read all of 2 Samuel chapter 11.

David fell by staying in the bed of idleness and not spending his solitude well, but Jesus Christ shows us a clear example of what it means to be productive in solitude.

Second Example: The Case of Jesus

> "And immediately the Spirit driveth him into the wilderness. And he was there in the wilderness forty days, tempted of Satan; and was with the wild beasts; and the angels ministered unto him." (Mark 1:12–13)

Jesus had just had a public experience. Many people saw how the sky opened above Him, the Holy Spirit descended in the form of a dove, and the Father's voice of approval was heard, but he was immediately taken by the Spirit out to the desert to be alone and tempted by Satan.

In contrast to David, Jesus was not in a palace. He found himself in the desert. He was not in a golden bed, but was surrounded by wild animals. Imagine this scenario of fasting and prayer! In my case, at least, if I had to find a place to fast for some days, I would choose a peaceful place, with spectacular nature and a beautiful countryside. But out Lord was not taken to such a place; he was pushed out into the desert, a place where no one wants to fast. There, in the midst of discomfort, after forty days without eating, Jesus was tempted by the obvious need to eat. However, in the middle of His solitude, His relationship with the Father and the Spirit was so strengthened that He was able to conquer Satan. Read this carefully: It is not so important to the enemy what we do in public—he is always waiting for us in private.

Let's be very aware that we are responsible for how we use our solitude. I encourage you to believe that your solitude consists of the most beautiful and powerful moments of your life with the Lord. Seek Him out, feeding your spirit with the Word and developing God's dreams that you be a blessing to others.

 Excessive Confidence

If there is a key principle for guarding our sexuality, it is prudence. Let's look at the case of Samson:

> "And it came to pass, when she pressed him daily with her words, and urged him, so that his soul was vexed unto death; that he told her all his heart, and said unto her, There hath not come a razor upon mine head; for I have been a Nazarite unto God from my mother's womb: if I be shaven, then my strength will go from me, and I shall become weak, and be like any other man." (Judges 16:16–17)

It is interesting to see that, although Samson played with sensuality just like Delilah, she used a strategy that many people use today to sleep with other people: winning their heart. This is especially common among many women, who offer sex in order to find love. The central issue with Samson was that he revealed his heart to her.

WHEN THE HEART IS ENSNARED,
EVERYTHING ELSE IS ENSNARED.

Excesses are bad and, sooner or later, they will destroy us. In this case, there was an excess of confidence, to the point that Samson confessed the secret of his anointing to Delilah. And after revealing his heart to her, he lost his strength. That is why my advice is this: Do not reveal your heart to just anyone. Remember, what is most valuable is your heart. "Keep thy heart with all diligence; For out of it are the issues of life." (Proverbs 4:23) I find it interesting that Solomon did not speak of sexuality, but rather of the heart. This is because when the heart is ensnared, everything else is ensnared.

If you have to open your heart to someone, do it with someone of your same sex, and someone who is more mature than you in the faith. If you are married, do not have deep friendships with another person who is not your spouse, nor with persons of the opposite sex. You cannot be chatting with just anybody, opening your heart to them and telling them about personal conflicts. You have your spouse for that, and you have your pastors, spiritual leaders, and mentors.

 Excessive Contact

> "And she made him sleep upon her knees; and she called for a man, and she caused him to shave off the seven locks of his head; and she began to afflict him, and his strength went from him." (Judges 16:19)

Although for some, having your head on someone's knees does not seem like anything serious, it was in Samson's case, because he was about to lose his hair—the sign of his anointing. And what does this make me think? That, often, small and silly physical contacts with someone who is "tripping you up" can be an open door to your destruction. It can be the detonator and the remote control that sets off the bomb and sends everything flying into pieces.

Let us be careful how we greet other people, especially those of the opposite sex. *Men*: It is better to be cold and distant than to seem predatory and inappropriate. If a woman is older than you, treat her like your mother; if she is your age, treat her like you sister; if she is younger than you, treat her like a younger sister or daughter. When there is purity, affection is an expression of Christ's love, not of passions disguised as friendliness. *Women*: You are like a beautiful field that must be fenced in on all sides, with a big sign in the middle that says "Private Property"; in other words, "This Space Is Not Available." You must be the one to set boundaries for your body and your heart.

Self-control is key to overcome excess. Self-control is the ability to govern ourselves—not by our own strength, because that is no more than willpower, but through the work of the Holy Spirit in us. Have you ever wondered why we need self-control? Because self-control is what will restrain that giant inside us—what will deactivate explosive devices.

A Carnal Mind

> "Then went Samson to Gaza, and saw there an harlot, and went in unto her." (Judges 16:1)

Wherever Samson went, carnality went with him, because he had a carnal and lustful mind; that is, Samson was a man who was easily dragged around by his passions. For this reason, when Jesus Christ spoke to us of sexuality, He did not speak of the bed, but rather of the mind and the heart, because clean or dirty sexuality begins in the mind. The Word of God reminds us of this:

> "Unto the pure all things are pure: but unto them that are defiled and unbelieving is nothing pure; but even their mind and conscience is defiled." (Titus 1:15)

Adventure

It is instructive that Scripture mentions the adventure that Samson had with Delilah, tricking her a number of times, "playing" with her about the secret of his strength (Judges 16:5–14).

He thought he was playing with Delilah, but the reality is that the enemy was already toying with him and had him in his hands. That happens to those who take an adventurous attitude toward sin. They say, "It's only a game; it's not serious," "It's only a song," "It's only a text," "It's only a meeting." But understand this: We do not fall when we put our heads on Delilah's knee; we fall when we play around with sin. The countdown begins when we start with the "little things" that open the door to lust.

 Lust

> "For the time past of our life may suffice us to have wrought the will of the Gentiles, when we walked in lasciviousness, lusts, excess of wine, revellings, banquetings, and abominable idolatries." (1 Peter 4:3)

The word *lust* refers to unclean and prohibited desires and passions. Lust is what feeds adultery, fornication, pornography, rapes, incest, homosexuality, and the rest. And here I wish to make a very pointed clarification: Many people criticize and judge others for sexual sins such as rape, homosexuality, incest, or pedophilia (which are certainly abhorrent in the sight of God), yet they ignore that those who practice fornication, adultery, or pornography are part of the same family, because these sins belong to the same root—lust—which leads them to this type of debauchery. Make note of this important information: Those who consume pornography are the primary sponsors of child prostitution. That's why it is key that we kill any hint of lust. This is the reason why Peter vehemently told us: "For the time [is] past!"

Perhaps someone who is reading these pages needs to say: "The time is past! I am not going to give more power to this bomb that has exploded inside me, blowing my purpose, calling, productivity, and family into a thousand pieces. I will not feed this time bomb any more, but rather, with the help of the Holy Spirit, I will disarm it."

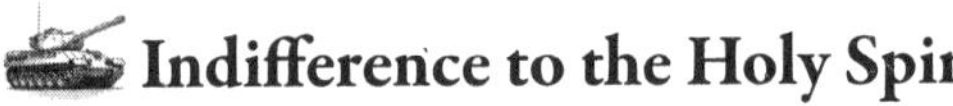

Indifference to the Holy Spirit

Samson told his father:

"Get her for me; for she pleaseth me well." (Judges 14:3)

On multiple occasions, Samson was called on to correct his behavior, but his reaction was always reluctant and obstinate, and although God used this to act against the Philistines, it did not change the fact that Samson had a willful inclination.

Making a comparison between David and Samson, we see that David fell further and his sin was more serious because he killed an innocent man, his trusted friend, for the purpose of sleeping with his wife. Nonetheless, when Nathan came to correct him on behalf of God (2 Samuel 12), he found humility and repented. And although he suffered the consequences, God raised him up stronger after his fall. For his part, Samson repented in the end, but died at the same time. Therefore, we can conclude that we will see Samson in heaven, but his purpose on earth was not completely fulfilled.

Battling with the Consequences

Although God forgives our sins, they still have consequences—especially moral sins, which are devastating and leave lasting consequences. Samson lost his eyes and became a joke to the Philistines.

> "But the Philistines took him, and put out his eyes, and brought him down to Gaza, and bound him with fetters of brass; and he did grind in the prison house." (Judges 16:21)

In David's case, the pain went even deeper. The child who was the fruit of his adultery with Bathsheba died (2 Samuel 12:14). In addition, his daughter Tamar was raped by his son Amnon (2 Samuel 13) and another son, Absalom, took vengeance by killing his own brother (2 Samuel 13).

Nonetheless, God was merciful and remembered Samson:

> "And Samson called unto the Lord: and said, O Lord GOD, remember me, I pray thee, and strengthen me, I pray thee, only this once, O God, that I may be at once avenged of the Philistines for my two eyes." (Judges 16:28)

God also gave David the opportunity to raise himself up again, sending the prophet Nathan to confront him (2 Samuel 12). When God confronts us and corrects us, He is showing us His mercy. Although it hurts and is shameful at first, later we will see the fruit of the love and mercy of God, who brings us to repentance.

I will finish this part of the armory by telling you that the weapon of the mercy of God is more powerful than our sin. Embrace His mercy.

Let's Go to the Trenches

For this exercise, you need to do something alone, and later do it with your group or trench partner.

Alone:

1. Make a list of the habits (good or bad) that you have when you are alone, and how much time you spend on them daily or weekly.
2. Add up this time.
3. Analyze the results these habits are producing in your life.
4. Identify which habits you must give up immediately, and which ones you can gradually give less time to.
5. Write a plan for replacing habits. For example: reading instead of social networking, gym instead of going back to bed. Include devotional time early in the morning or late at night.

With Your Trench Partners

If you feel free to express your answers and engage with them, I encourage you to do so.

1. Share which habits you have when you are alone that have helped you grow.
2. Share what God has taught you in this chapter about overcoming sexual immorality.

Important: Do not advance to the next battlefield before going through the trench!

CHAPTER EIGHT

RUN, FORREST, RUN

We have walked through the battlefield of the body in the moral area, but we cannot disconnect from the reality that we are the house of God, so our body must not only be sanctified, but also cared for so that it remains healthy.

I don't know if you remember the brilliant, epic movie *Forrest Gump*, starring the great actor Tom Hanks. The film begins at a bus stop, when Forrest starts to tell the story of his life to the people sitting next to him on the bench. The protagonist has a mild intellectual disability, and when he was a child, had to use orthopedic devices due to motor problems with his legs. He walked with difficulty, which caused the neighborhood children to reject him and make fun of him. All of them except Jenny, who became his best friend and great love.

While he continues narrating his childhood, we see a very moving scene. One time, when Forrest was walking clumsily next to Jenny, some boys started to bother him, throw rocks at him, and push him down. At that moment, Jenny saw the danger and urged him to run using a phrase that is engraved on the hearts of everyone who has seen the movie. She shouts: "Run, Forrest, run!" Hearing the girl's voice, he finds strength he didn't know he had and does something he had never done: He starts to run so fast that the orthopedic devices break. From this moment forward, Forrest becomes a great runner, achieving many goals that are shown in the rest of the movie.

I will never erase this scene from my mind. I will hold onto it for the rest of my life, because it taught me two things:

- First, nothing is impossible for those who hear the voice of our God. More than once, I have heard Him say: "Run, David, run! Let's go! Overcome your limits!" and this has brought me to achieve goals that I thought I could not achieve.
- Second, from the moment Forrest discovered his physical potential, he began to run. In his youth he became a great athlete, the fastest on his university team. Later, he went to the Olympics and was the fastest, and even during war, his ability enabled him to save lives. His ability had such an impact that he ran across the United States and inspired many to follow him.

This movie teaches us about the importance of keeping ourselves strong and caring for our bodies—for our own good, and for the good of others. For me, the shout, "Run, David, run!" is a challenge to me to take care of myself and run like a good athlete, not only spiritually, but also physically. I have to be ready to run to what God has called me to do, and my good health is an ally in getting there.

I can recall a good number of people who were tremendously talented, with exceptional abilities and brilliant, long careers—but they stopped running. They no longer had the strength or health to fully accomplish their missions. They probably thought that the body, good health, good physical conditioning, exercise, and a healthy diet were not important—that the only important thing was their calling and the mission they had to carry out because, "God will take care of the rest." So, many were gone early from this earth because they did not take care of themselves.

This brings me to ask myself certain questions: How many more books would have been written? How many more buildings would have been built? How many more social and missionary projects would have been carried out? How many churches would have been established? How many movies, television series, creative projects, and designs would have been carried out if only there had been this awareness that the body is the house of God?

OUR DAILY TASK, AFTER GIVING GOD THE FIRST PLACE IN OUR LIVES, IS WORKING CONTINUOUSLY ON THE WELL-BEING OF EVERY ASPECT OF THOSE LIVES.

In the Christian world, we've often stigmatized and nearly condemned caring for the body, and therefore caring for our health, saying that it is merely a reflection of what we carry inside ourselves.

I would like you to reflect on this: Many people criticize the care of the body, but at the same time, they wish to be healthy. This is like having a car in disrepair and criticizing those who have well-maintained cars—but also longing for the car owned by the person we are criticizing. In other words, many criticize those who take care of their bodies and their health, while secretly wanting to have the same health those people enjoy.

God does not want us to be overly invested in outward beauty, but He does want us to take care of this house—His house—where he lives. Scripture speaks of this when it asserts that our "body is the temple of the Holy Spirit" (1 Corinthians 6:19). When we care for our bodies in a healthy and holistic way, we not only care for ourselves, we honor God and reflect our devotion to Him.

Our daily task, after giving God the first place in our lives, is to work continuously on the well-being of every aspect of it. This is what this book is about: taking you through every chapter, represented as battlefields, to lead you to victory in every area.

In this particular chapter, we will focus on caring for the body, the physical part of ourselves, since, as I said earlier, we are the house of God. The apostle Paul said:

> "Know ye not that ye are the temple of God, and that the Spirit of God dwelleth in you?... the temple of God is holy, which temple ye are." (1 Corinthians 3:16–17)

Your body is not simply the place where your spirit lives temporarily—it is the residence and dwelling place of the Holy Spirit. Therefore, just as with temples, you must treat your body with respect. Caring for the well-being of our body and our health is a personal decision and responsibility.

The Word of God says:

> "But the path of the just is as the shining light, that shineth more and more unto the perfect day." (Proverbs 4:18)

As good, wise, and sensible people, we must remember that all of the good work we do in and by ourselves will also be reflected in the way we take care of our health and our bodies.

The great wise man Solomon gave a very serious exhortation:

> "Keep your body healthy." (Ecclesiastes 11:10 NLT)

Let me remind you that maintaining a holistically healthy body—spiritually, morally, and physically—is our responsibility.

God has given us the power to make decisions. We have been created with free will. Biblically, this is known as "free choice"—the ability to choose between what builds us up and adds to us, and what destroys us and subtracts from us. In other words, free will is the right to choose between good and evil and to act according to our will, turning our daily actions into a reality in our lives.

The desire of our heavenly Father is that all of our works be good. If we apply this to the care of our bodies, the wish and will of God is not that we are full of ailments, illnesses, and living a mediocre physical life, but rather that we are strong, healthy, and examples of good bodily stewardship. Remember that people watch us before they listen to us.

We must remember that everything we do daily becomes reality. That is why we must think about the benefits or consequences attached to everything we do for ourselves.

Speaking of caring for the body, did you know that the only place our soul has to live in this world is our body? A question arises for me when I reflect on this: How very necessary do you think it is, then, that we treat it properly?

As we pursue that well-being, we will encounter distinct adversaries that will get in the way and do everything possible to prevent us from reaching our goal. It is important to know them and identify them, because we fight with them daily. Do you want to know what they are? There are many adversaries that will try to prevent you from taking care of yourself—but in this chapter, we will focus on one of the most common.

 The Peril of the Hammock and the Attack of Laziness

There is always a rest area in every camp, and many of these feature hammocks where people can rest. Personally, I love hammocks. They are incredible for a perfect afternoon of rest, especially when the weather is nice. However, I have a few memories that illustrate the peril of the hammock.

When I was a child, we often went to visit my aunt and uncle in the plains of Casanare, Colombia. They had set up many hammocks, where several family friends and neighbors would rest. Beer in hand, they would begin to drink, and would stay there for hours and hours, to the point that many of them began to get sick due to their sedentary lives. For many of them, rather than resting, the tendency was simply to lounge in laziness.

Now I want to clarify that this doesn't mean that hammocks are bad, because the same things we say about hammocks, we could say about sofas or beds. The problem is abusing rest and sinking into a culture of idleness, carelessness, and neglect on which *sloth* feeds.

Sloth is known as one of the sins that God most detests and is defined as negligence or an attitude that prevents doing things that need to be done. If we allow this adversary called sloth to enter, it will take charge of filling our minds with false arguments for avoiding the care and well-being of our temple. Each day when we wake up, we must be ready and equipped to resist the "attack of laziness."

 How Does This Adversary Attack Us?

First, thoughts opposed to the will of God come to our minds. We can identify them because they are thoughts that destroy and do not edify; thoughts that carry discouragement, passivity, and excuses with them, ultimately leading to negligence. They lead to the law of least effort.

I would like to introduce you to some of the allies of sloth:

- **Fallacies:** These are "fables or fairy tales" that come into our minds and distract us and cause us to lose focus on discipline. Sloth only imagines things, but it does not achieve anything.
- **Idleness:** This is nothing more than wasting time on things that subtract rather than add; that do not edify but destroy; that do not shape us but deform us and lead us to a place of high unproductivity and, ultimately, lethargy, emotional illness, and even physical sickness. I have seen the damage idleness causes to people, homes, organizations, and nations.
- **Lack of discipline:** Sloth is never, ever in favor of discipline. It's interesting to observe that sloth often disguises itself with good, making us think we deserve a rest on the sofa, or a break in our healthful diets, or a pause in our exercise routines. But in reality, sloth is a weapon the enemy uses to destroy.

Satan loves to see us discouraged, doubtful, hopeless, low on self-esteem, wasting time, unfocused, destroyed, disoriented, directionless, planless, lacking objectives and any sort of courage. In a nutshell, Satan wishes us to be completely apathetic toward the plan that God has for each of us.

A PERSON WHO DOES NOT TAKE CARE OF THEIR BODY BECAUSE THEY ARE TOO LAZY TO IMPROVE THEIR HABITS IS A PERSON DESTINED FOR PAIN AND ILLNESS.

It is not in the Enemy's best interest for any human being to be focused, happy, and fulfilling their life's purpose. That's why the first target of sloth's attack is our mind. If we allow laziness to take up residence in our minds, we give way to the destruction of our dreams, plans, hope, vision, and projects.

A person who does not take care of their body because they are too lazy to improve their habits is a person destined for pain and illness. How many chronic conditions and illnesses do we suffer due to lack of diligence?

 What Does the Word of God Say about Laziness?

The book of Proverbs, in particular, is full of wisdom regarding laziness and offers warnings for the lazy person.

> "The slothful man saith, There is a lion in the way; a lion is in the streets. As the door turneth upon its hinges, so doth the slothful upon his bed. The slothful hideth his hand in his bosom; it grieveth him to bring it again to his mouth. The sluggard is wiser in his own conceit than seven men that can render a reason." (Proverbs 26:13–16)

> "The soul of the sluggard desireth, and hath nothing: but the soul of the diligent shall be made fat." (Proverbs 13:4)

> "The hand of the diligent shall bear rule: but the slothful shall be under tribute." (Proverbs 12:24)

There must be no place for laziness in the life of a Christian. While laziness is a lifestyle for some, it is also a temptation for all. This is why we must overcome the Enemy's attack every day, staying focused on the search for well-being in every area of our lives. And in this specific case, sloth damages our health and prevents the diligent, timely care of our bodies. However, the great news is that God has a reward for those who overcome this enemy.

I invite you to discover the weapons that we have in Christ to defeat laziness and jump out of the hammock.

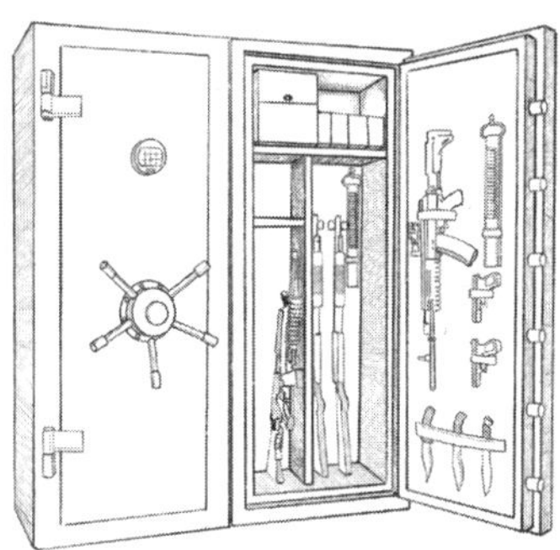

Let's Go to the Armory

The Bugle

The military uses the bugle to awaken and call the soldiers. How great it is to have someone who blows the bugle loudly to awaken us from sleep so we can jump out of the hammock and defeat laziness!

The beautiful part of this call from God is that it is not based on judgment, scolding, or offense, but rather on love and care. The love we give our bodies—God's house—is tied to the value we place on ourselves. That's why the loud sound of the trumpet coming from what you're reading in this chapter, which may get under your skin, has one purpose: to affirm in you who you are, and from there, to motivate you to build a strong and healthy life in every area. I hope that what you have read so far helps wake you up and makes you more intentional.

A person who knows his value in Christ loves and protects every area of his life, since he sees it as God sees it. For this reason, the first thing you must know is who you are for God.

- You are His special treasure (Malachi 3:17)
- You are beautiful (Genesis 1:27)
- You are loved (John 3:16)
- You are valuable (Matthew 10:31)
- You are chosen (John 15:16; Thessalonians 1:4)
- You are special (Jeremiah 31:3)
- You are fearfully and wonderfully made by God (Psalms 139:14)

For a soldier in Jesus Christ, who is clear about his identity before God, it is not possible for Satan to rule him. When we value what we are in God, we will value everything He gives us. We value our time and multiply in blessing everything that has been given to us.

The Clock

Another weapon we have is the proper use of our time. In order to help soldiers be punctual and adhere to established schedules, military bases install synchronized clocks and use a system of measured time periods. This provides many advantages, including organization and the maximization of efficiency. It leads to good use of time.

The Word of God says: "To every thing there is a season" (Ecclesiastes 3:1–8). And within the time given to us each day, we must set aside time for exercise and proper nutrition. Caring for our body is a wise choice because, if we are strong spiritually, mentally, and physically, we will weaken sloth, instead of it weakening us. We must be intentional and disciplined in this work.

The apostle Paul exhorted us:

> "Redeeming the time, because the days are evil." (Ephesians 5:16)

The words that are translated as "redeeming the time" in this verse come from the Greek term *exagorazo*, which means exactly that. That is, it's not just about not wasting time, but also about redeeming it, extracting good from it.

There are three types of people: those who *lose* time, those who *waste* time, and those who *redeem* time. Those who redeem or extract good from their time are those who maximize it. This is key for keeping us physically healthy and strong, because two hours in front of the television are not going to redeem your time like one hour running or exercising. When we are intentional in the use of time for our care, we will be more efficient.

To develop this chapter, and with regard to all the weapons you will read about below, I have leaned on the support of doctor María del Mar Cabarcas, a specialist in holistic beauty and anti-aging, in addition to being a great friend of our family. From her experience in care of the body, she explained two essential weapons for us.

The Garden (Dr. María del Mar Cabarcas)

Any soldier ready to confront a battle needs to take care of his nutrition, so that his body will be strong and ready for the fight. The rigorous work of troops on combat missions requires a menu rich in proteins, carbohydrates, fats, vitamins and minerals—one that can endure high temperatures and can even be eaten cold.

We are not the exception. As we have been learning throughout this book, the battles we confront every day require us to be especially careful in how we feed ourselves. This is the concept re-enforced by Doctor Cabarcas with this weapon called "the garden":

> The Scriptures state that on the third day of creation, as described in Genesis 1:11–13, God brought forth plant life on the Earth. He ordered: "Let the earth bring forth grass,

the herb yielding seed, and the fruit tree yielding fruit after its kind." (v. 11). And thus, obedient to His command, the earth exploded with an abundant blossoming of greenery.

This creation of plant life on the third day was critical for establishing the basis of sustenance and survival for all living beings. The diverse types of plant life created included herbs, grasses, and fruit trees. These plants provide food and nutrition for animals and human beings and play a vital role in maintaining the balance of nature.

The importance of this act of creation is obvious in the fact that plants have been flourishing on the Earth since that time. They are not only a source of sustenance, but also contribute to the beauty of our surroundings. They provide oxygen, absorb carbon dioxide, and support the intricate web of life on our planet.

The creation of plant life marks an essential moment in the Biblical narration, highlighting a loving and intentional God who carefully designed and provided for His creation.

If each of us limited ourselves to eating only what God gave to feed us, we would not suffer from many of the illnesses that exist today, but the hand of man has distorted the foods that were created by God for our well-being. Sweets, fried foods, processed flours, refined oils—these did not come from God, and they are killing us. Reading these words, some might say, "This is not very spiritual," or "Where does the Bible say this?" and will close themselves off to these ideas, but let me give you some biblical examples to uphold these concepts.

- God fed the people of Israel very well in the desert. In Exodus 16, we see that God gave them manna in the morning and quail in the evening. Think about this: The manna had all of the nutrients necessary for Israel to be nourished (not full, but nourished). Do you know what quality of food is necessary to live for forty years in the desert, not just walking, but also fighting enemies and surviving hard times? You need to be well-fed for that.

- John the Baptist, who also lived in the desert, ate honey and locusts, and he did not die of "locust-itis." God gives us what is necessary so that we are well-fed.

What would happen if we substituted fruits for sweets, delicious fresh vegetables for fried foods, and roots for processed flours? If you were to eat poultry or fish, your health, I assure you, would be different. God gave us everything necessary for us to live a quality life on this earth.

It is scientifically proven that our stomach is considered our "second brain," because a healthful diet also supports the well-being of our emotions and thoughts. Who would have thought! And truly—isn't it amazing how good we feel when we eat well?

I feel that I am following God in caring for the body He gave me, instead of when I choose foods that destroy my body or sicken it. Have you felt the burden on your conscience when eating poorly? It is terrible, because it is a silent and progressive destruction of our temple.

I remember meeting a worship leader—a very talented man, an incredible musician who loved God—who very much enjoyed a popular soft drink. For years, his diet consisted of a liter of this soft drink, accompanied by bread. It was not long before he had critical diabetes that took him before his time.

I encourage you to substantially improve the quality of your diet, because wise people eat well and take appropriate servings. And once you are eating well, there is another important weapon: exercise.

Exercise

This weapon is basic for any soldier. The website *Atleta Táctico* states: "Military training must provide its members with abilities that enable them to successfully overcome great physical exertion and moments of adversity... Your condition as a soldier must be as perfected as possible, since the physical ability of the unit is limited to that of its weakest members."[1] This means that you need to be in shape, not only for yourself, but also for the well-being of all of those who fight the battle with you or depend on what you do.

Regarding the weapon of exercise, Doctor Ana María Cabarcas told us the following:

> It is not so much age as physical inactivity that most impacts the ability of people to do things for themselves. The lack of physical activity also results in more visits to the doctor, more hospitalizations, and increased use of medications for many illnesses.
>
> Did you know that exercise contributes to your happiness? After prayer, exercise is one of the greatest keys to a happier life. Do you know why? Because in addition to the physical and health benefits we gain, the four "happiness hormones" are released every time we exercise.

God loves for us to exercise, stay healthy, and shine.

Think about it. Does it make a father or mother happy or sad when their children take care of themselves? Happy, of course! I feel happy when I see that my children do not allow garbage into their minds or bodies. When that happens, we can watch them build a better version of themselves—because they are aware of the importance of holistic care. The same thing happens with God for us.

Let's remember that the body is the only place we have to live in this world. We should exercise every day, and we know that this will bring blessings to our lives.

Just like our spiritual life, the body must be worked on in different areas. Each day of the week, should be dedicated to strengthening a specific muscle group. Here are some simple routines that can greatly help you care for your physical health:[2]

- Monday: arms and back
- Tuesday: glutes and cardio
- Wednesday: legs, core, and cardio
- Thursday: arms, back, and cardio
- Friday: legs, glutes, and cardio
- Saturday: cardio
- Sunday: rest

We need strategies to keep our muscles strong. If you're not used to exercising, the best recommendation is to start gradually, but little by little, we should increase our efforts. The best way to strengthen our muscles is to perform three or four rounds with repetitions that go from highest reps to lowest reps, but each time with more weight. For example:

- Round 1: 21 repetitions with a 10-pound weight.
- Round 2: 15 repetitions with a 15-pound weight.
- Round 3: 10 repetitions with an 18-pound weight.
- Round 4: 7 repetitions with a 20-pound weight.

This pushes muscles to work, grow, and get stronger. And strong muscles help ensure a healthy old age and a high quality of life.

If we read biblical history, we can see that, in the past, human beings lived longer and enjoyed very good health. If we analyze this history carefully, we can also see that they fasted, walked a lot, did not use screens, cellphones, tablets, or computers. In addition, everything they ate came from the earth—fish from the sea, birds, and other species. So, the Bible contains the true formula for anti-aging and caring for the body.

Let's eat what our Father gave us on the Earth for our sustenance. Exercising daily and being in the presence of God guarantees us marvelous health. Jesus Christ, our Lord, is an example to follow. He himself physically prepared His body to endure the great suffering of the cross for us. He had the strength of the Father, but He exercised to be strong in order to achieve His mission. He didn't go to the gym, but He did travel through villages, towns, and cities.

Only in God can we live a fully balanced life. Not just one day, but every single day. Remember that we all have the same twenty-four hours as a gift from the Father, so let's use them well.

The wisdom to make excellent use of what God [1]has given us—especially our time, which is a great treasure—comes from Him. A daily rhythm of well-being gives us courage, strength, confidence, and hope that all will be more than well in our lives.

Keep in mind that for this well-being plan to last, we must be very intentional every day in overcoming the "sluggard" within us, so it won't take over. And for that, it's very important that you spend some time in the trenches.

Let's Go to the Trenches

Our only safe place is in God, because only from Him do we receive the very best for each of our lives. That is where we find balance, true fulfillment, peace that surpasses understanding, light, guidance, wisdom, hope, and our true identity. In His presence, we recognize our failings and receive strategies to grow ever closer to holiness, fulfilling His purpose.

Our priority must be to maintain a constant relationship with the Father and His affairs here on earth. The only way to resist the enemy is by putting God first—always.

However, the people and activities with which we surround ourselves contribute to our physical and mental well-being. Therefore, having friends who add to our lives and motivate us is part of success. This is key for encouraging yourself every day.

Studies show that we are the average of the five people we spend the most time with. So, choose wisely who you have around you. Be intentional about those activities that bless your life: conferences, sermons, groups, retreats, a church with healthy doctrine—and share your activities with people who love to take care of themselves in every area of their lives. This will bring you motivation in this arduous battle in search of holistic well-being.

Assignment:

- Get together with one or two fellow soldiers and agree to engage in exercise routines like running or bike riding (if they also happen to be from your team in the trench, so much the better). If you are married, this is very good therapy to do as a couple.
- Take a few minutes to pray together.

We are in the home stretch of this adventure. If you have crossed each battlefield, I want to congratulate you, because I am sure that God will give you victory.

Important: Do not advance to the next battlefield before going through the trench! See you there!

CHAPTER NINE

THE SILENT ENEMY

We have gone through a very powerful journey, and I am sure that you have seen the hand of God working in your life. So, I hope you are prepared to enter this new battlefield, where you will confront a silent enemy—one that does not come alone to attack you and cannot be perceived by our physical senses. I am referring to the spiritual forces of evil.

I have a friend who is retired from the United States Army and served in several wars in Iraq and the Middle East. He is always telling me incredible stories. In one conversation, he spoke to me about something he experienced at the very beginning of his time as a soldier. This is what he told me:

> A soldier feels oppressed from the moment his basic training begins. From that first day, a process begins to break down this new recruit and build him up again, turning him into a full-fledged a soldier, a war machine. This entire transformation is overwhelming. You feel oppressed twenty-four hours a day, seven days a week, because the process is designed so that, in the end, you become an individual programmed to follow orders and instructions, executing them in detail without questioning anything. Throughout that regimen, they condition you to operate under high levels of stress and pressure without allowing it to affect your performance. The level of oppression throughout the process is so high that people often fail to complete it.

Throughout this training they also emphasize the development of a sense of belonging to a group—*esprit de corps*, in French—so that everyone supports one another and in this way minimizes that sense of oppression. That feeling of comradery, along with the development of a high degree of motivation, will last for all the years of a military career and will be a key element in tolerating such levels of oppression.

Now, having become soldiers, we go to the battlefield and submit ourselves to situations that are intense for the following reasons:

- The responsibility to carry out the assigned mission exactly as designed.
- The tension produced by having soldiers under your charge—and the worry that not all of them will survive.
- Seeing other soldiers or civilians badly wounded, dismembered, or dead.
- The pressure to do everything possible to avoid collateral damage (wounded or deceased civilians).
- The physical strain caused by the weight of military equipment you carry (approximately forty to eighty pounds, or more), the extreme temperatures, and the few—or nonexistent—opportunities to rest or get enough sleep.
- Fear of being wounded or losing one's life.

Since my friend is a firm believer in his faith, I asked him how, as a Christian, he faced such intense oppression. He explained:

> For the Christian soldier, in addition to that oppressive burden, there is spiritual oppression, which I think is even more intense. I can say that the environment of death and desolation weighs on you, and it's very disturbing.
>
> On one occasion, I felt so overwhelmed that I went to a military chaplain for advice. He understood and explained to me that, in the territory where we were then located,

> great battles had been fought since the beginning of time. For this reason, the spiritual burden there was more intense. From that day, I understood that, in the face of all this oppression, my most effective weapon was my faith and prayer.

Upon hearing him, I could easily relate what he was telling me to the oppression that many of us experience as soldiers of the Lord, because—keeping things in proportion—this is what the oppression of enemy spiritual armies feels like. I am sure that, as soldiers of the Lord, all of us at some point have faced the persecution of the Enemy. And if Christ is in us, we can better perceive both the spiritual world and the Spirit of God, as Paul said:

> "But the natural man receiveth not the things of the Spirit of God: for they are foolishness unto him: neither can he know them, because they are spiritually discerned." (1 Corinthians 2:14)

For someone who does not have Christ, the spiritual world does not exist or is simply considered "a strange energy" that moves in the environment—what many today call "vibes." Millions of people are oppressed by the Enemy, but they don't realize it because they are not spiritual. That is, they do not have a spiritual awareness of things.

Perhaps, like me, you can identify with the face that before coming to Christ you were insensitive to spiritual realities, but now, having your eyes spiritually open, you can perceive beyond what is simply seen. It is also possible that you feel that before knowing Jesus life seemed "easier," without so many attacks against you—and that after your conversion the pressures and attacks became stronger. Well, this has two good explanations:

- The first is that, when we become children of God, we begin to be shaped in His image. To do this, He uses difficult circumstances that forge our character and bring us to a new level of faith, knowledge of Christ, resilience, dependence, and victory (and if don't think so, ask Job, who became an expert on the subject). The author of Hebrews said it well: "For whom the Lord loveth he chasteneth, and scourgeth every son whom he receiveth" (Hebrews 12:6).
- The second is that many of these attacks and pressures come because Satan, the Enemy of our souls, has his artillery ready to attack us.

It surprises me every time I see how many Christians are foreign to the spiritual world, and some have even come to believe that demons do not exist, despite the fact that the apostle Paul clearly described to us the battle we are undertaking and confirmed that our fight is not against persons, but rather against these spiritual entities.

> "For we wrestle not against flesh and blood, but against principalities, against powers, against the rulers of the darkness of this world, against spiritual wickedness in high places." (Ephesians 6:12)

Now, this is not about being afraid, nor about blaming the devil for everything that happens to us, nor about seeing him everywhere. Many Christians go to the opposite extreme and see the devil everywhere, but don't see God anywhere. There are those who speak more of the devil and his demons than of God, giving him a greater role than he really has. This is about balance and showing how this Enemy of our souls operates.

What Paul wanted to say is that we must elevate our perspective of spiritual warfare and understand that there are spiritual forces of evil operating in the air and atmosphere with a clear purpose: to obstruct and destroy the work of God in the world and in those who surrender themselves to Him.

 Destructive Drones

Most of the discoveries and inventions of the last centuries have been astonishing creations with the potential to bring solutions to humanity. However, many of them have been misused by the wrong hands, becoming, in many cases, weapons of destruction.

In chapter 4, I told you about a type of drone used as a protective weapon, called "the anti-mine drone," and I shared how a young man managed to use drones to locate anti-personnel mines. Even so, these same drones, used by someone with destructive intentions, can be lethal.

A while ago, I read an article in the Euronews site about the use of drones in the most recent wars in Europe and the Middle East. In that article, professor of the International Campus for Safety and the Defense of Spain, César Pintado, said that drones, "are at the forefront of military revolution, a technological revolution, and a revolution in how to wage war and understand it."[1] Drones are becoming increasingly fast, undetectable, destructive, and affordable—instruments "that governments are using to inflict pain on the other side," affirmed Abishur Prakash, the CEO of Geopolitical Business.[2]

In the same way that drones are used in military operations to identify enemy positions, mark the place that should be bombed and attacked, or correct the position in the case of a bomb gone wrong, at the spiritual level, there are also "drones" that strike us across different missions and from different fronts. How do these drones operate?

 Silent attacks

Let's be realistic. The enemy does not say, "Listen, I'm going to attack you—get ready to defend yourself." On the contrary, his schemes and assaults generally come by surprise, especially when we are careless.

Consider what our Lord Jesus Christ said to Peter:

> "And the Lord said, Simon, Simon, behold, Satan hath desired to have you, that he may sift you as wheat." (Luke 22:31)

Peter did not understand what Jesus was telling him, nor was he ready for it. However, what Jesus stated came to pass down to the smallest detail. This confirms for me that if Peter was attacked and "sifted," we will not be free of such attacks.

Although it may sound strange, everything I have explained throughout this book is a spiritual truth: We are soldiers. We form part of the army of God. Therefore, it is naïve and irrational for a soldier to think that he will not face battles, but he will instead go on vacation and enjoy an easy life. Sadly, this happens with many believers who think that Christian life is like a rose garden or Disneyland, where everything is beautiful and pleasant, and protected within a bubble where nothing can touch us. And let me clarify: In Christ, we are safe—but we are not trophies in a glass case that no one touches, but rather soldiers on the battlefield. We can have the assurance that, although we are attacked, we will not be destroyed. If we remain firm in the middle of these spiritual battles, we will see victory—and the victory is that Christ will be forged and formed in us.

If you go back and read Luke 22:31, you will be able to note something very interesting: Peter was viciously attacked by Satan, but just as with what happened with Job, the devil had to ask God's permission to have access to him. This clarifies two things for me: The first is that no child of God is under the authority of Satan—nor of his demons—and the second is that Satan can indeed attack the children of God. Jesus Christ did not say to Peter: "But I have asked him not to touch you", but in the next verse He said, "but I have prayed for thee, *that thy faith fail not*" (Luke 22:32). In other words, "The attack will come, but My prayer is that when this happens, your faith will make you stand firm."

WE ARE SOLDIERS. WE FORM PART OF THE ARMY OF GOD. EVEN THOUGH WE MAY BE ATTACKED, WE WILL NOT BE DESTROYED.... THE VICTORY IS THAT CHRIST WILL BE FORGED AND FORMED IN US.

I hope this truth lights up your life in such a way that you will not fear the attacks of the enemy but remain firm in the face of those threats. Many of us fall or weaken in the face of these attacks instead of being strengthened by them.

This is what happened with Peter. He overlooked the attack that Jesus Christ warned him about. And why? Because he thought it wouldn't happen to him—that he would not fail the Teacher. Pride was the root of this, just as it is within us, along with our immaturity, when, relying on ourselves and not on the grace that is given to us, we say, "No one is going to touch me" or "Even though everyone fails, I will not fail." This is why God allows some attacks, not to destroy us, but rather to make us aware of how much we need His grace and how dependent we must be on Him.

So, if you are under attack, remember that this is part of the battle. However, the Enemy operates at an even higher level that I will explain next.

 Oppression

There is a tremendous story that Luke narrated about a woman with a hunchback who had been suffering for nearly eighteen years. I do not know if you can imagine the situation this woman had suffered for so long—the pain, the shame, the burden that it was for her. When she met Jesus, she was healed, but Jesus said the following:

> "And ought not this woman, being a daughter of Abraham, whom *Satan hath bound*, lo, these eighteen years, be loosed from this bond on the sabbath day?" (Luke 13:16)

This was Jesus' response to the hypocritical Pharisees who criticized Him for healing on the day of rest. But it also reveals that this woman's illness was the product of a spiritual force over her.

It should be noted that spiritual oppression works in a similar way—like a hunchback that keeps a person from standing upright. So, the issue changes here, because this I more than a simple attack or trickery; it is spiritual oppression that can be caused by demons or spiritual bonds.

You may be asking the same questions I once asked myself: Can a Christian be oppressed? And my answer is: What The Scriptures show us is that a believer cannot *live* under the oppression of the enemy, but can experience *moments* of spiritual oppression. I am talking about moments of oppression due to external pressures, which do not come from within because of a hidden sin or from the practice of sin, but rather are a result of attacks that become oppressive over time. Remember what I told you happened in Elijah's heart through the words of Jezabel? This is exactly what I'm talking about.

In 1 Kings 19, Scripture shows us how those words so deeply disturbed the heart of the man of God that fear entered him and he went on the run. Elijah's oppression was so great that he asked God to kill him. And he didn't just think it, he said it out loud. We certainly see that this was a diabolical plan against the man of God, and that he fell into this trap.

How many times has it happened that, suddenly, we feel depressed and unmotivated, we don't want to learn or do anything and, "all of a sudden" we start to feel greatly discouraged? How often, "out of nowhere," do we start to fight with our spouse or speak harshly to our children, as though we had entered some strange cycle of anger? We must have discernment, because often this is spiritual oppression caused by external forces—that is, from demons who have been assigned to destroy our lives, our marriages, and our families. Be careful! These signs may indicate that spiritual forces of evil are seeking to oppress us and confuse us so that God's plan will not unfold in our lives.

Demonic Possession

> "And when he was come out of the ship, immediately there met him out of the tombs a man with an unclean spirit, who had his dwelling among the tombs; and no man could bind him, no, not with chains: because that he had been often bound with fetters and chains, and the chains had been plucked asunder by him, and the fetters broken in

> pieces: neither could any man tame him. And always, night and day, he was in the mountains, and in the tombs, crying, and cutting himself with stones." (Mark 5:2–5)

Here we see a clear example of someone demon-possessed. In this case, the characteristics were clear, and you might even think they seem a bit extreme, but the Bible shows us another case with a girl who was also possessed, yet whose appearance and behavior seemed "normal." Let's see how the physician Luke, the author of Acts, told it:

> "And it came to pass, as we went to prayer, a certain damsel possessed with *a spirit of divination*, met us, which brought her masters much gain by soothsaying: The same followed Paul and us, and cried, saying, These men are the servants of the most high God, which shew unto us the way of salvation. And this did she many days. But Paul, being grieved, turned and said to the spirit, I command thee in the name of Jesus Christ to come out of her. And he came out the same hour." (Acts 16:16–18)

Luke is clear in affirming that she "had a spirit of divination," which means that she was inhabited by demons—she carried a demon inside that made her move in a supernatural world. And it is important to emphasize here that not all of the supernatural world is of God. The demoniac of Gadara also moved in a supernatural sphere, and the wizards of Egypt knew how to move in a supernatural dimension, changing rods into serpents by the power of demons. For that reason I reiterate: The fact that most demons are not visible does not mean they do not exist.

Many Christians doubt whether demon possession is real and avoid speaking of this because they do not want to sound like mystics or fanatics, or they do not want to "scare" people. What they are really doing is allowing the Enemy to have his way in the lives of those who believe that everything is behavioral or psychological. Let me clarify: I do believe psychology has its proper place when used wisely and on biblical foundations, and I also believe not everything is demonic in origin. However, many close themselves to spiritual reality—perhaps because they have seen exaggeration, imbalance, or sensationalism—and as a result they ignore the central text of this chapter:

> "For we wrestle not against flesh and blood, but against principalities, against powers, against the rulers of the darkness of this world, against spiritual wickedness in high places." (Ephesians 6:12)

Once again, we are invited to lift ourselves up and become aware of the spiritual world that moves above us—in the heavenly realm and in the air (whether in cities, nations, towns, or districts)—and also of those sent to destroy families, churches, and ministries. We must be aware of the spiritual battle we face every day.

I want to clarify again that a believer can indeed be attacked, but not possessed, because darkness and light cannot coexist in the same place. When Christ dwells in someone, demons cannot inhabit that person.

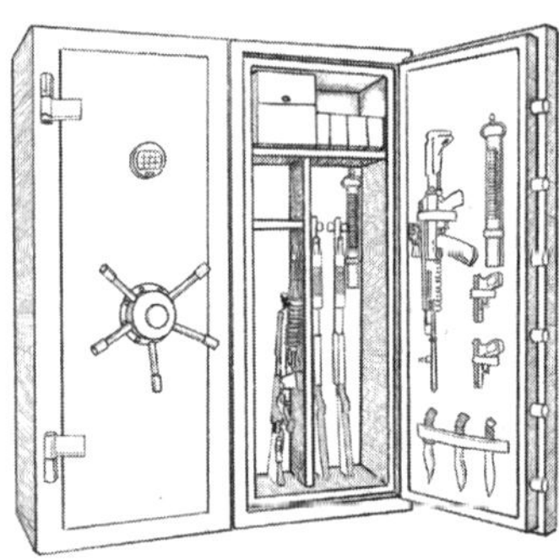

Let's Go to the Armory

 The Iron Dome

Israel's famous Iron Dome (also known in Spanish as the *Cúpula de Hierro*) is not a protective cover in the sky, but rather a network of missiles placed in strategic locations throughout the country. When the system detects an incoming projectile, the interceptor missiles launch and neutralize it before it reaches its target. The way this system works is fascinating.

First, a radar detects any incoming missile up to seventy-five kilometers from its target. This signal is sent to the missile silo, which, in turn, fires missiles to meet the destructive projectile in the air, stop it, and destroy it. The explosions are heard, but it is very difficult for the incoming missiles to reach their targets, since the system is 90 percent effective.

In the same way, we can neutralize any attack or scheme of the Enemy, because remember: Attacks are inevitable, but we can stand firm and spiritually armed to defend ourselves.

Here is how Paul told us this:

> "Finally, my brethren, be strong in the Lord, and in the power of his might. Put on the whole armour of God, that

> ye may be able to stand against the wiles of the devil." (Ephesians 6: 10–11)

The Spanish word artimañas ("wiles") comes from the Greek term *medsodeía*, which means "to lie in wait with tricks or deceit". And this is precisely the strategy of the enemy: to use tricks, deceit, and artifice. For this reason, Scripture affirms that we need to strengthen ourselves in the Lord, since it is definitively He who gives us victory. Thus we can state that our first and most important shield is Christ and His work for us.

Let's see what the apostle Paul said:

> "And you, being dead in your sins and the uncircumcision of your flesh, hath he quickened together with him, having forgiven you all trespasses; blotting out the handwriting of ordinances that was against us, which was contrary to us, and took it out of the way, nailing it to his cross; and having spoiled principalities and powers, he made a shew of them openly, triumphing over them in it." (Colossians 2:13–15)

What did Christ do on the cross to give us victory and set us free?

- He pardoned our sins.
- He canceled "the handwriting of ordinances" that was against us and nailed it to the cross.
- He disarmed principalities and demons, triumphing over them.

Our spiritual freedom is consummated on the cross. So then, following this reasoning, what must we do to be free?

1. Believe in the sacrifice of Christ and His work on the cross.

> "If the Son therefore shall make you free, ye shall be free indeed." (John 8:36)

I observe with great concern that today, in many churches, deliverance is spoken of as if it were a matter of psychological therapy or an exercise with a number of steps we must take—something like, "do this and do that"—unconsciously ignoring and nullifying Christ and His work.

As I said earlier, I think that psychology, carefully applied and grounded in Scripture, is a necessary tool. But it is not what gives us freedom. It is the person of Christ who sets us free, not any therapy or any exercise with a series of spiritual steps that we follow. Of course taking steps of obedience is important, and seeking help is essential. But it is by faith in Christ and His work that we are free. So, once I believe in the sacrifice of Christ, I have the authority to renounce all sin I have committed or will have committed and, in Him, embrace the new life.

Now then, how can we remain free? Our priority must not be to concentrate on being perfect or on not sinning again, but on living in Christ and in union with the Holy Spirit—not according to our sinful nature or our flesh.

> "There is therefore now no condemnation to them which are in Christ Jesus, who walk not after the flesh, but after the Spirit." (Romans 8:1)

IT IS THE PERSON OF CHRIST WHO SETS US FREE, NOT ANY THERAPY OR ANY EXERCISE WITH A SERIES OF SPIRITUAL STEPS THAT WE FOLLOW.

When we live in Christ, we are not empty—we live in His abundance. What nurtures us, strengthens us, and makes us powerful in God is a life filled of His Word.

> "For the word of the Lord is right; and all his works are done in truth." (Psalms 33:4)

When the Word of the Lord feeds us every day—when it is our guide, our bread, and our priority—we truly stand firm. When we read with care, study with interest and depth, meditate with calmness and humility, and apply His Word with faith and obedience, neither Satan nor his demons will have access to our lives. Jesus defeated Satan with—and by—the Word, and the latter fled from Him. Thus, we ourselves can be more than conquerors using the Word.

The beauty of communion with God is that He has given us our Comforter, the Holy Spirit, so that we may live a fruitful and abundant life. Our communion with the Holy Spirit will ensure protection against attacks and a door sealed off against silent enemies.

Christ is and will be sufficient for living a life in freedom, and we have His Word and His Spirit to keep us in this freedom into which we have been freed.

Let's Go to the Trenches

Remember, the trench is the safe place where you, along with your group of soldiers with whom you have read this book, share what you've learned. But if you are alone in the trench, don't worry—the Holy Spirit will be with you.

Here is the guide from the trenches for this battlefield:

- What are the differences between attack, oppression, and spiritual possession?
- Share an experience you have had related to these three types of spiritual situations.
- If you are being attacked, oppressed, or feel that you need to be set free, share this with your group, and seek out your pastor or spiritual leader so they may pray for you.
- Fast for at least one day to weaken your flesh, break any spiritual chains, and strengthen your spirit. Be sure to have your leader or pastor supervise you and pray for you when you finish.

CHAPTER TEN

AFTER THE BATTLE

We have arrived at the last chapter of this spiritual military journey, and we have learned many valuable concepts that will help us emerge victorious from each of our battles. The questions now are these: What now? What happens to a soldier after a battle?

An article in the publication *The Conversation*, entitled *"The Psychological Cost of having to Fight in a War"*, tells us the following:

> During the Second World War, terms such as "battle fatigue" and "combat stress reaction" were used to describe a variety of behaviors resulting from the stress of battle. The most common symptoms were fatigue, slowed reaction times, indecisiveness, disconnection from their surroundings, the inability to prioritize, and, on some occasions, a "freeze response."
>
> For this reason, three principal mental disorders are spoken of: post-traumatic stress disorder (PTSD), depression, and traumatic brain injury. There are obvious mechanisms that link each of these conditions with specific experiences in war. Unfortunately, these disorders are often invisible to the eyes of others... Furthermore, after reviewing a number of investigative studies, a large variety of symptoms and psychological syndromes have been detected in populations in conflict.[1]

What does this mean? That our battle is not over when we win the war. After their return home, soldiers suffer a variety of mental and emotional problems and we, as soldiers, are not exempt from these. There is an enemy who continues to stalk us even after the victory. That enemy is lack of rest.

In this chapter, I want to teach you about the importance of rest, because just as a soldier arrives home to rest after a long battle, so we, too, must rest. Perhaps you are thinking: *But, David, my battles are not over, I can't wait until this spiritual or emotional battle ends, because I don't believe it will ever end,* and you would be partially right, but it is precisely there that our strategy lies: We need to learn to rest *in the middle* of battle, to live *in rest,* to produce *from rest,* to serve *from rest,* to fight *from rest.* Thus, as stated in the letter to the Hebrews, we must enter God's rest and live there.

> "Let us therefore fear, lest, a promise being left us of entering into his rest, any of you should seem to come short of it.... For we which have believed do enter into rest, as he said." (Hebrews 4:1, 3)

 Super Busy

The author Tim Chester wrote a book entitled *The Busy Christian's Guide to Busyness* [2], in which he described our apparent inability to rest, which is piously excused due to ecclesiastical tasks. In his book, he said it this way:

We Christians are as exposed as anyone else to every kind of external pressure. And we may even have a few more. We have made "workaholism" into a virtue. The time we dedicate to the family is, without a doubt, important for us. But church meetings and responsibilities have to be added to this. On this subject, Robert Banks gives the opinion that, "with regard to time, we Christians are in a worse situation than others"...

Previous generations divided time on the basis of a whole. Today, we quantify it in minutes... In real time, every second counts. The maximum effect must be squeezed out of every minute. And, since it is impossible to hold back the time that escapes us, we have recourse to machines as a viable alternative. Two simultaneous options. Divided screen. Multi-tasking option. Voicemail messages. Imaging fusion on screen. You don't have to miss a thing. In fact, we cannot even allow such a thing....

For a while, I was convinced that my problem with competing concerns was going to be transitory. But as time passed, it became clear that that would not be the case. Things do not change by themselves. And trying a little harder in order to be able to stop later didn't work either. As soon as we finish with one thing, another pops up in its place—like sand when we dig at the beach. If we truly want to find a solution to multitasking, the only possible way out is to choose and prioritize.

A Forced *Stop*

When we, as a society, went through the COVID pandemic in March 2020, the whole world was paralyzed. It is hard to admit that I believe my emotions were paralyzed as well. Seeing all the plans I had for that year collapse within a month, I started to feel panic and despair. I had settled into an accelerated pace: appointments, ministry, church, family—everything on top of a temperament that is predominantly sanguine. So, to suddenly find myself forced to stop dead in my tracks left me feeling lost in the midst of such stillness.

My wife Diana is different. She is happy at home, enjoying her surroundings. And although I also like spending time at home, I am much more accustomed to being on the move, going out frequently, never stopping my body—and certainly never stopping my mind. And that is when the problem started. My mind was always thinking about what was coming up and could not enjoy the present from being too focused on the future. I began to walk a path I would never have chosen, one that started in my mind and then manifested itself in my body.

Visits to the clinic close to my house became more frequent. Whenever I felt like I was drowning, I blamed it on COVID and ran to the emergency room, only to have the tests confirm that my lungs were fine. My symptoms were so frequent that one day the doctor said to me, "You are wasting time I should be spending on patients who really have breathing problems. Your lungs are fine. What you have is anxiety, and you need a different kind of treatment."

Anxiety? But I prayed, I worshiped, I preached—how could this be possible? Over time, I understood that the other kind of treatment the doctor referred to is called rest. Such a simple thing was almost impossible for me, since my life was caught up in a barrage of activities that was doing me harm. I didn't think that stopping was a good thing. I don't know if the same thing has happened to you, but I grew up with the mentality that if you were resting or didn't do anything for a day, it was practically a sin. I thought that it didn't matter what day it was, I always had to be doing something. I didn't know that the sin was not doing nothing, but rather ignoring the command to rest and thereby harming my physical, mental, emotional, and even spiritual health.

During those four months of lockdown, I had to learn to rest—and I'm still learning—but that time of crisis helped me become more intentional about rest.

So, allow me to share three important lessons with you that will help you make the most of and enjoy your times of rest.

- **Sometimes doing nothing is actually doing more.** Your body is much more productive when you rest. According to health experts, rest is essential for our cognitive well-being, regulates our breathing rate, improves attitude, improves peoples' mental, cardiovascular, cerebrovascular, and metabolic health. This is why you are not more productive when you spend too many hours without a break. You are more productive when you take the time you need to recharge the batteries of your body, mind, and spirit.
- **Rest is not just about sleep, it is also about disconnecting.** Changing activities, reading a good book, enjoying nature, engaging in sports, listening to music, or separating oneself from technology for a few hours, are some of the actions you can take intentionally in order to rest, even though you are not sleeping. Choose to incorporate activities or stillness that bring refreshing moments to your spirit, not those that exhaust you or wear you down. Choose to disconnect from everything that robs you of peace and rest, and connect with the Word of God. In that Word, you will find the principles and promises that will bring holistic rest to your body, mind, and spirit.
- **Fill yourself up so you can give.** The devotional, *Making time to rest* [*Dedicar tiempo al descanso*][3] created and provided by the platform YouVersion, puts it this way:

  The reason we need rest is that we have been working or using energy in some form. And just because we may have learned how to rest and feel rested, doesn't mean

> *we will stay that way. We will go back to work. We will help others again. We will be emotionally exhausted again.*
>
> *It is not all about rest for its own sake. We rest and relax to be able to work again. There is a beautiful ebb and flow to work and rest; to being full in order to be able to give.... Just as our bodies need enough hours each night to recover, our spirits also need this. We cannot hope to have a strong and vibrant spirit without investing in it. We cannot expect that a one-week vacation will sustain us for months and months. We must make daily deposits in our account in order to endure. And we need to be paying attention when many withdrawals have been made... Every day, we wake up with a certain amount of mental, emotional, and physical energy. When we have poured out everything we have to give, we must rest. When we are empty, there is less of us, which hinders His work in our lives.*
>
> *Come close, stop, and rest. This is the good and right moment to be filled with the Spirit of God.*

The directions are clear and simple: **We need to rest.** Farmers let the earth rest so that the fields will be more productive at harvest. Animals rest in hibernation. Nonetheless, for us it is continuously more difficult to find space for rest in our tight schedules. The *multitasking* culture of doing many things at once, always being busy, active, "productive," and tired, is applauded and considered a synonym for success by the world, and a signal of being the "most Christian" in the church. Something so easy has become extremely difficult for us.

This reminds me of the story in the book of 2 Kings. It tells of Naaman—a general of the Syrian army, a man loved and valued by the king of that nation for the many victories he won for his people—having leprosy, an illness that could not be cured despite all of his titles and medals. In his despair, Naaman listened to the advice that a Hebrew maid gave his wife and, after some "bureaucratic maneuvering," decided to visit the prophet Elisha.

Arriving at the prophet's location, Naaman became very angry, because not only did Elisha not receive him, but he also told him through his messenger that the reason was this: "And Elisha sent a messenger unto him, saying, Go and wash in Jordan seven times, and thy flesh shall come again to thee, and thou shalt be clean" (2 Kings 5:10). The proud general, respected by many, could not understand this apparent snub from the prophet, much less that the solution to his problem was so simple. But look at what happened:

"But Naaman was wroth, and went away, and said, Behold, I thought, He will surely come out to me, and stand, and call on the name of the Lord his God, and strike his hand over the place, and recover the leper. Are not Abana and Pharpar, rivers of Damascus, better than all the waters of Israel? may I not wash in them, and be clean?

"So he turned and went away in a rage. And his servants came near, and spake unto him, and said, *My father, if the prophet had bid thee do some great thing, wouldest thou not have done it?* How much rather then, when he saith to thee, Wash, and be clean? Then went he down, and dipped himself seven times in Jordan, according to the saying of the man of God:

"...and his flesh came again like unto the flesh of a little child, and he was clean." (2 Kings 5:11–14)

What am I trying to tell you with this? Naaman found his health by obeying an easy instruction that he had resisted at first because of all the arguments in his mind. Likewise, we fill ourselves with arguments against obeying God's simple instruction to rest: "Who has time to rest?" "if I don't do it, no one will," "I have to work day and night," "I will feel guilty if I don't do it," "I can't ignore this opportunity," "I can't say no to that." And so, this becomes one more day, one more concern, one more yes, that causes us to say no to the voice of God. We prefer complicated, elaborate, structured, and expensive solutions, instead of paying attention to the simple instruction of our Father who tells us: "It's time to rest. Enter into my rest."

So, my question for you is: Are you ready to enter into the rest of God? As I said before, we need to learn to rest after battles, but also *in the middle* of them. We may live, produce, serve, and fight our battles—the seen and the unseen—*in rest* and *from rest.*

CONCLUSIONS

Let's Go to the Trenches

As you have seen on the battlefield, the trenches have been key. We need to open our hearts, since each one of us is a universe full of ideas, feelings, thoughts, dreams, concepts, memories, desires, lost and won battles, and this space has helped us to share our battles with fellow soldiers who find themselves on the same battlefield.

I want you to know that, for me, this book has been a trench where I have also been able to open my heart, so that you may simply identify yourself with this man who, although he is a pastor, carries his scars and wounds, but continues to learn from every battle lived.

This project, *Hidden Battles,* has cost me many sleepless nights, much prayer, much study, but the most important thing is that I have understood the reason why of many experiences that I have had. God has allowed me to go through such things so that today I can share with you, from my heart, what He has taught me through His Word and what He has allowed me to learn not only through battles won, but also through those I have lost. In this space that is the trench, and with you as my comrade in arms,

I share with you that, by writing every page of this book, I have won a hidden battle.

I now invite you to sit down in this trench, no longer with your comrades, but rather just you and the Holy Spirit, and to take this opportunity to internalize some principles. As the author of this book, guided by God, I am here to ask you key questions that I want you to answer in all sincerity:

- What have you learned about the character of God from this book?
- What things have you seen in yourself after reading this book that you had not perceived or realized before?
- What sins, habits, and attitudes is God calling you to abandon?
- What spiritual virtues have you learned by reading this book?
- What commands is God calling you to obey?
- What promises must you believe and embrace?
- What examples is God calling you to follow or avoid?
- What resolution or commitment to the Lord are you making?

Now, pray this with me:

> *Heavenly Father, thank you for giving me the great privilege of knowing you. Thank you for the battles that I have been able to experience until today, because you have been with me in the middle of every painful process, and you have not only guarded me, but also healed me to be more like Christ.*

Today, I surrender. Yes, I surrender myself to you, I surrender my desires and passions, weaknesses and strengths. Today I ask for your forgiveness if I have had destructive or unproductive habits, if I have opened my heart to that which does not edify it, if I have not built a biblical mind. Today, I take strength from Jesus Christ and from the power of His strength, and I ask you, heavenly Father, that I may be that soldier who is firm in the rock that is Christ, clothed in all of the armor of God. Today, I believe with all my heart that, in the battles of my life, I will see the hand of God, and I will grow in the image of Christ, because my victory is to be more like Him!

Thank you, Father, for loving me so much.

In the name of Jesus Christ, my Lord and Savior, amen.

If you would like to, send me your comments about your experience with this book. You can do this by accessing the QR code on this page. I would like to know how this journey has been for you. I also encourage you to share it on your social media networks—Feel free to tag me on Instagram (@davidscarpetaoficial), or upload it to your social media history with photos of your notes.

Thank you for allowing me to be your comrade in arms.

Until next time, soldier!

NOTES

Chapter 1: The Sniper

1. Maritime component of the first special operations force of the Navy of the United States.

Chapter 2: Grenades in my Mind

1. John Calvin, *Institutes of the Christian Religion*, Faith Alive Christian Resources, January 2014.

Chapter 3: Target Practice

1. Sun Tzu, *The Art of War* (New York: Basic Book, 1994).

Chapter 4: Heartbreaking Mines

1. Jonatan Pedernera, "Estudió en un sótano y se convirtió en el mejor alumno del mundo", ADN + Una buena noticia, April 22, 2023, https://adnpositivo.com/estudio-en-un-sotano-y-se-convirtio-en-el-mejor-alumno-del-mundo/.

Chapter 6: Beware of the Hulk!

1. In Spanish, Reacción de Estrés ante la Operación de Combate. It is also known as *combat fatigue* or *shell shock*.

2. Information taken directly from *Military Review*, official journal of the United States Army, written by Major Tim Hoyt, PhD, component of the United States Army Reserve, Captain Christina L. Hein, Phd, United States Army. https://www.

armyupress.army.mil/Portals/7/military-review/Archives/Spanish/Q1-2022/Q1-Hoyt-2022/Hoyt-SPA-Q1-2022.pdf.

3. In Spanish, Unidad de Transición del Guerrero, used to relieve stress related to operations in the combat zone.

4. Journal *Military Review*, "How to address behavioral health impact", Lieutenant Colonel Christopher Landers, United States Army. https://www.armyupress.army.mil/Journals/Edicion-Hispanoamericana/Archivos/Tercer-Trimestre-2017/Como-abordaren-la-salud-conductual/

Chapter 8: Run, Forrest, run

1. "Military Training. Physical preparation in the army". *Tactical Athlete*. Last accessed on: August 6, 2024. Available at https://atletatactico.com/como-es-el-entrenamiento-militar/.

2. The routines suggested here are generic and for general information, and should not be used as a substitute for the evaluations or recommendations of a professional qualified in the field. Visit a professional if you need specific help.

Chapter 9: The Silent Enemy

1. Euronews, "How drones are conquering the battlefield in Ukraine's war?", June 6, 2023. Last accessed on: September 23, 2024. Available at https://es.euronews.com/2023/06/05/como-los-drones-estan-conquistando-el-campo-de-batalla-en-la-guerra-de-ucrania#:~:text=Los%20drones%20tienen%20misiones%20como,kil%C3%B3metro%20o%20centenares%20de%20metros.

2. *Idem*.

Chapter 10: After the Battle

1. https://theconversation.com/el-coste-psicologico-de-tener-que-combatir-en-la-guerra-179428.
2. Tim Chester, *Cristianos superocupados* (Barcelona: Editorial Andamio, 2013) [The Busy Christian's Guide to Busyness, London: Inter-Varsity Press, 2006].
3. https://www.bible.com/reading-plans/16169-making-time-to-rest